Three Seasons of Summer

gardening with
annuals and biennials

Three Seasons of Summer

gardening with
annuals and biennials

Ethne Clarke
photographs Marijke Heuff

Picture acknowledgements

Marijke Heuff would like to acknowledge the following gardens and kind cooperation of the garden owners who allowed her to photograph: Huis Bingerden, Angerlo, Holland, pages 4, 24–5, 57, 72, 80–1, 88–9, 93, 118–19, 126, 127, 131, 133 (centre), 133 (bottom), 149 and 163; Mrs A. Broekhuis, Holland, pages 25 and 98; Farmgardens, Switzerland, pages 11, 82 (left) and 108–9; Mrs W. Gramsbergen, Holland, page 6; Ineke Greve, Holland, pages 9, 29, 42 (left), 90–1, 99 (bottom) and 116 (top); Mr and Mrs Groenewegen, Holland, pages 17, 70 and 110–11; Mrs L. Goossenaerts, Holland, pages 116 (bottom); de Hagenhof, Holland, pages 44, 45, 47 and 66; Hortus, Amsterdam, Holland, page 115 (left); Irene Jansen, Gieten, Holland, pages 73 (right) and 138; Monet Gardens, Giverny, France, page 155; Nursery Coen Jansen, Dalfsen, Holland, page 130 (centre); Nursery de Kleine Plantage, Eenrum, Holland, pages 54, 71, 83 (right), 85 (right), 113, 119 (right), 140–1, 144 (left), 146 (centre), 150–1, 159, 162 and 164–5; Nursery Piet Oudolf, Hummelo, Holland, pages 67, 68–9 and 154; Ton ter Linden, Ruinen, Holland, pages 22, 28–9, 30–1, 33, 34, 35, 38 (top), 46, 51, 53, 55, 56, 60, 61, 62–3, 72–3, 74–5, 76–7, 87, 96, 101, 102–3, 120, 124–5, 136 (right), 137 (right), 140 (left), 142 (top, centre and bottom), 146 (bottom), 151 (right), 152–3, 156–7 and 160; Mrs G. Lauxtermann, Holland, pages 18, 38 (bottom), 104–5, 114 (right) and 161; Ineke Lambregts, Holland, page 110 (left); Palace Het Loo, Apeldoorn, Holland, page 123; Garden designed by A. Noel, England, page 130 (bottom); Nursery Overhagen, Velp, Holland, pages 2, 12, 13, 32 (left), 42 (right), 43, 48–9, 94–5, 99 (centre), 128 (left), 128–9, 129 (right), 130 (top), 146 (top) and 147; The Old Vicarage, Norfolk, England, pages 40–1; Priona Gardens, Schuinesloot, Holland, page 134; Garden designed by Els Proost, Holland, page 27; Gardens Mien Ruys, Dedemsvaart, Holland, pages 82–3, 84 (left), 84–5, 114 (left) and 143; Smerpertuin, Hippolytushoef, Holland, pages 14–15, 16–17, 24, 28, 32 (right), 100, 107, 116 (centre), 117, 122, 132, 133 (top) and 144–5; Sahin seeds b.v., Alphen aan den Rijn, Holland, pages 1, 8, 23, 39, 50, 59, 78 (left), 78–9, 79 (right), 99 (top), 112, 114 (left), 135, 136 (left), 137 (left), 148, 150 (left) and 158; Sÿtje Stuurman, Holland, pages 86, 97, 111 (right), and 114 (right); Street gardens, Amsterdam, Holland, page 26; Theetuin, Weesp, Holland, page 106; Mrs P. G. Voûte, Holland, pages 19 and 141 (right); Parc Weihen Stephan, Germany, pages 58 and 139; Castle Wÿlre, Holland, pages 20–1; and Ethne Clarke, England, pages 36–7 and 52–3.

A DAVID & CHARLES BOOK

First published in the UK in 1998

Copyright © David & Charles 1998
Text Copyright © Ethne Clarke 1988
Photographs Copyright © Marijke Heuff 1998

A catalogue record for this book is available from the British Library.

ISBN 0-7153-0807-6

Printed in Italy by Lego SpA
for David & Charles
Brunel House   Newton Abbot   Devon

CONTENTS

INTRODUCTION

Among the most pleasant memories of flower-garden things are often those of annual or biennial plants: tall and splendid Stocks in a farmhouse garden . . . Snapdragons on old garden walls, and bright marigolds everywhere; Hollyhock lines, Sweet Pea hedges, and Mignonette carpets; Evening Primrose, Poppies, Sweet Scabious and Sweet-williams.

William Robinson

The English Flower Garden

As Robinson so correctly observed, annuals and biennials are planted in most people's memory garden. When recalling my first efforts at garden-making, it is the spiky black zinnia seeds sown in wonky rows at our back door that come first to mind, a thought quickly followed by recollection of the thrill I had from watching each vibrant bloom open then fade slowly to seed, which was patiently gathered to provide the next season's magic show. It seemed nothing short of miraculous that from such unpromising

beginnings, an exciting plant could grow; it remains, too, a source of great satisfaction – and wondrous mystery.

Annuals provide some of the brightest and longest-lasting flowers in the garden and they bloom over a long season, beginning with sky-blue forget-me-nots in spring and carrying on into early autumn with the papery everlastings so popular with flower arrangers. They are often used with exotic tender perennials to create the vivid (sometimes shocking) floral displays seen in public parks and amenity gardens. This is a legacy of the Victorian fashion for carpet-bedding, and the careful production and regimented layout demanded by such a scheme ensures that each plant receives the growing conditions annuals prefer: light, moisture and space to grow without competition.

In 1868, the editors of *The Cottage Garden* magazine published *The Garden Manual*. This small book was aimed

at the growing number of hobby gardeners among the middle-class, white-collar workers who were moving into the fast developing suburbs of Britain's main cities. Annuals, they remark, 'are now too often considered as mere weedy things', but the small section devoted to these simple flowers compares them favourably to bedding plants, and provides a number of suggestions about ways to ensure a succession of blooms.

Frequent dead-heading is the first tactic, followed by inter-row successional sowing and careful thinning of young plants. More ambitious is the reserve garden of annuals sown in pots, or (and this is quite intriguing) on thick pieces of turf with plugs removed and filled with seed compost and then sown with the desired successional crop; they remark that this method is suitable for small gardens 'where freshness and frequent changes are desirable, and where labour is an item never complained about'. (I doubt such gardens exist today.)

The faded black and white photograph of the Glasgow garden of my husband's great-uncle Matthew J. Clark (without an 'e') shown above reveals him to have been a formidable horticulturist, and he may well have been an uncomplaining reader of *The Garden Manual*; he was clearly an outstanding practitioner of carpet bedding. In the approved fashion of the time, the garden is girdled by

PREVIOUS PAGE *Annual and biennial flowers are among the most vibrant in the garden and contribute to the colour scheme over a long period. Bright yellow* Bidens *'Golden Eye', shining lilac-pink* Lavatera trimestris *'Silver Cup' and a scattering of button-flowered everlastings (*Xeranthemum annuum*) are typical of the clear, bright colours of annual flowers.*

PREVIOUS PAGE INSET *Ghostly pale colours are also part of the annual palette, and none is more spectral than the soft white of the old-fashioned Canterbury bells (*Campanula medium*).*

raked gravel paths, centred on a tiny garden house (complete with trim lace curtains). A formal scheme of square and rectangular beds was planted up with what looks like every colourful tender annual, from ageratum to zinnia. Zonal pelargoniums, agave and cordylines were used as 'dot' plants to give height, while dahlias and chrysanthemums for cutting were tucked into their own beds; the cornerposts were topped by inverted flowerpots to attract and thereby trap earwigs.

Hardy annuals were clearly not of interest; just as the authors of *The Garden Manual* explained, these simple flowers required no skill to raise and for a newly fledged homeowner with pretensions to grandeur, hardy annuals were too redolent of the rural cottage garden. But it was the hardy annuals' simplicity, their willingness to self-sow and their ability to mingle gracefully and naturally with perennials and shrubs that helped the race to endure. William Robinson and Gertrude Jekyll both advocated the use of hardy annuals, and in her book *Annuals and Biennials* Miss Jekyll included a number of ideas for mixed plantings of perennials and ephemerals. I particularly like Robinson's suggestion for foxgloves: 'when any ground is broken up for fence-making or rough planting . . . scatter a few seeds of the white and other pretty kinds and leave them to take care of themselves'. He goes on to say that there are many ornamental grasses that can be treated as annuals and have the benefit of carrying their flowers through the winter – a prophetic remark when you look at the gardens of leading modern designers and plantsmen like Piet Oudolf, Henk Gerritsen and Mark Brown in Europe, and Oehme and Van Sweden in the USA.

The contemporary trend for naturalistic gardens is in the relaxed style of the early 20th-century Arts and Crafts gardens, but taken a step further. Where once the mixed flower borders would have been set off by neat lawns and box edgings, instead the grassy matrix contains annuals like quaking grass (*Briza maxima*), squirrel tail barley (*Hordeum jubatum*) and foxtail millet (*Setaria italica*) dotted through with California bluebell (*Phacelia campanularia*), corn poppies (*Papaver rhoeas*) and toadflax (*Linaria*). Such a planting recalls the richness of a flower-strewn meadow and attracts a diversity of insects and birdlife which add another dimension to the garden.

OPPOSITE *Great-uncle Matthew was an avid horticulturist, as his bedded out garden in Glasgow shows; laid out behind an unassuming bungalow, the plot is now a garage forecourt.* Tempus fugit.

ABOVE *Ribbons of French marigolds (*Tagetes*) and* Salvia coccinea *'Lady in Red' bedazzle a formally bedded-out centrepiece of dahlias in a trim Dutch vegetable garden.*

The gardens shown throughout this book make the best possible use of annuals for structure and colour; any perennials take second place to the largely self-sown annual and biennial display, the beauty of which continues as the seedheads form and the foliage bleaches. In particular, the garden of the Dutch watercolourist Ton der Linden, demonstrates what is possible by exploiting flower and leaf colour, shape and texture to create the most naturalistic yet carefully orchestrated of colour gardens. This is gardening in a simple and direct fashion; many of the plantings are self-sown, with the balance maintained by judicious thinning of the seedlings early in the season, selective cutting back and removal of only the shabbiest plants.

Piet Oudolf is one of Europe's outstanding plantsmen and a specialist in grasses. His nursery and garden at Hummelo in Holland are a showcase for the many fine grasses he has introduced and a display ground for the perennials and annuals best suited as companions to the grasses, grown in a habitat-sensitive manner.

A Dutch garden which I find particularly inspiring is the Priona Garden at Schuinesloot, made by Henk Gerritsen and inspired by his observations of nature. This is a garden composed almost entirely by natural incident, gardened with the lightest of touches. How often have you heard it said that a self-sown plant has 'put itself in exactly the right place', and that 'nature is the best gardener'? The evidence for this is Henk's garden; certainly he introduced the plants to the site and delineated the various garden areas, but beyond that initial 'kick-start', it appears that all is as it would be and wants to be, and form and texture take precedence over colour – just as they would in nature.

LEFT *The many uses for annuals and biennials is not confined to the flower garden; here ebullient and exotic bouquets have been made of dahlias, a tender perennial that we grow like an annual.*

ABOVE *Bunches of cottage garden favourites like mallow, zinnias, salpiglossis, larkspur and starry dill flowerheads, can be gathered for indoor decoration.*

LEFT *Like a living* millefleurs *tapestry, this meadow is a colourful mix of fine grasses and self-sowing annual flowers. The term* millefleurs *means 'thousand flowers', and describes the floral motif often seen in medieval woven hangings where, against a dark background, individual flowers were shown in detail as fine as the craftsmen's art would allow. Lilies, daisies, lily-of-the-valley, periwinkles, strawberries, primroses, and other common flowers were dutifully rendered, providing a benign pastoral setting for the central figures – most typically ladies in elaborate costume and their chevaliers, with the occasional unicorn passing through.*

Here the mix in ribbon beds either side of a grassy path includes snapdragons, linaria in shades of peach and rose, blue Phacelia tanacetifolia, *Shirley poppies, corn poppies, scabious and cornflowers. Many of these annuals are favourites of bees and butterflies, so the meadow is alive with more than vibrant colour. Seed must be sown in well-prepared soil that is free of grasses and perennial weeds and raked to fine tilth. Once the floral carpet is established it should self-sow, although some of the stronger sorts will eventually dominate unless, by careful thinning and planting, the gardener helps the more reticent flowers to take hold.*

SUMMER
BEGINS

The culture of flowers implies the lightest possible kind of garden labour; only, indeed, enough to give an interest in its effects . . . the culture of flowers is exactly in the happy medium between what is too hard and what is too easy.

Jane Loudon
Gardening for Ladies

As soon as the daffodils begin their earnest flowering, pushing back the winter blankets, you can look out at the garden and see the flecks of cobalt-blue that by the beginning of summer will have swelled into a frothy sea of forget-me-nots. These are among the most useful of late spring–early summer plants; they make brilliant groundcover beneath early-flowering shrubs like currant bushes, lilac and mock orange. Their tight tuffets of foliage knit together to form weed-smothering blankets between emerging perennials, and the vibrant blue flowers are the most welcome sight.

Forget-me-nots epitomize the ease of gardening with annuals; they will sow themselves with cheerful abandon, creating a fine blue haze against which tulips and late spring bulbs can show off, then making groundcover until the summer plants take the stage. Later, faded clumps of forget-me-nots can be simply swept away – but only after shedding their seed. It is the ability of hardy annuals to self-sow that guarantees their place in the naturalistic garden plan, for as long as they are suited to the conditions of the site and to each other, they can be used to create the ornamental matrix through which summer-flowering perennials will grow in their time.

However, there is another side to annual gardening, one that takes some effort to realize to its full potential, and which, in spite of what Mrs Loudon advised, takes some effort to produce a result – the complete annual garden, in which all the flowers are from the hardy or half-hardy tribe. But when the planning has been carefully considered, the plants well grown and the soil adequately prepared, few sights can compare.

Modern gardeners have been conditioned into thinking of perennials as being the plants that provide the most colour in the garden, yet earlier generations appreciated annual flowers almost as much. Once the fairly painless propagation process is complete, working with annuals to create colour effects is in some ways easier. They generally flower over a longish summer season, their range of colours is enormous, and the prolific nature of the flowering permits some quite saturated colour effects which can be exploited in Jekyll-like gradations, or more casually treated to provide a grand explosion of colour to make, for example, a welcoming carpet in front of your house.

If you take to annual gardening seriously, collect as many catalogues as you can. I know one enviably organized gardener who has a reference tool assembled from photos snipped from catalogues, pasted on cards, annotated and filed by colour. I'm always tempted to shuffle the cards to draw a random planting – a kind of floral lottery!

ABOVE *California poppies (*Eschscholzia*) are excellent naturalizers. The dwarf* E. caespitosa *'Sundew' makes an especially good flowering groundcover among perennials with oversized leaves like this variegated hosta.*

OPPOSITE *The delicate blue of the common forget-me-not (*Myosotis sylvatica*) is one the finest tints of the late spring–early summer garden. The cultivar 'Royal Blue Improved' is taller than usual and has especially fine deep blue flowers.*

PREVIOUS PAGE *The awe-inspiring sight of a garden devoted entirely to hardy annuals shows precisely why generations of gardeners have devoted time and energy to their cultivation. Cosmos, lobelia, snapdragons, poppies, cornflowers and ox-eye daisy are just a few of the dazzling flowers creating a spectacle in this modern version of a traditional flowery mead.*

LEFT *Annuals can also be used to perform specific design tasks in the garden plan; many of the low-growing sorts, such as pompon-flowered forms of the common lawn daisy (*Bellis perennis*), sweet alyssum (Lobularia), dwarf forms of ageratum and non-trailing sorts of lobelia — in all its shades from white to darkest blue — make charming low borders along pathways. In a formal garden, the beds within the defining shrub borders can be filled with annuals, like the white bellis, sweet alyssum and violas used here in alternating areas of a formal parterre. As the season progresses, the colour scheme can be altered.*

Alternatively, annuals can be used to create a knot pattern in a formal garden design; there is evidence that in the gardens of the Italian Renaissance, annuals were used where traditionally we are advised to use dwarf box or some other low-growing herb. Imagine substituting brightly coloured annuals for evergreen hedging and weaving the multi-coloured threads in and out of each other. The effect could be quite giddy, but might be just the sort of lively touch your garden needs.

Ribbons of low-growing annuals need not be confined to the outer edges of the flower beds, and can be grown in a sinuous trailing line among taller-growing perennials or beneath shrubs to make groundcover.

There are many annuals plants suitable for use in the middle of the border, as fillers or as blenders, or where height is needed: larkspur (*Consolida*), rose mallow (*Lavatera trimestris*), common marshmallow (*Malva sylvestris*), tickseed (*Coreopsis tinctoria*). ornamental sages and nicotiana. These have loose, open shapes and work in well among shrubs and perennials, but I also find that tall-spiky plants can be the most effective shape for mid-border use – foxgloves are top of the list.

Plants with this mid-height stature are extremely useful as 'blenders'. If you select a colour that will harmonize with the main theme of the planting, the annual flowers, which will dot and dash between the perennial clumps, will serve to consolidate the main colours. Similarly, taller-growing annuals can be used as eye-catching companions for mixed plantings of perennials and shrubs. The star in this league is *Verbena bonariensis* – strictly speaking a perennial, but at its best treated as an annual. It has tall – up to 1.5m (5ft) – stems that are whippy-thin and sparsely foliated. At the tip of each lanky stem is a cluster of tiny, bright purple flowers. I first saw this growing in a derelict iris garden said to have been planned by Gertrude Jekyll; the path between the beds was sunken so that the iris flowers appeared at head-height and the verbena had seeded itself heartily amidst the

iris rhizomes and in a few other select places around the garden. It was there I realized the wonderful effect to be gained by viewing a herbaceous planting through a thin screen of annual stems and tiny flowers.

Cleome, or the spider flower, is another good, tall-growing annual mixer, but its distinctive flowerheads assure it a rather more prominent role than the one allotted to the verbena. It assertive appearance is best exploited by using it in repetitive order rather than scattered willy-nilly throughout the garden; this is generally true of characterful and statuesque annuals.

SOWING YOUR PLANTS

As soon as the last threat of winter frost has faded, annual activity in the flower garden can begin in earnest – and while the sowing and planting out of hardy and half-hardy annuals and biennials is not as strenuous as some sorts of gardening, it nonetheless demands attention to detail.

Hardy annuals can be sown in late spring or early summer, when the soil is beginning to warm and it is well-moistened by spring rain – the ideal conditions for healthy, steady growth.

ABOVE *Love-in-a-mist is one of the finest early-flowering hardy annuals; its soft blue flowers look like Elizabethan lace collar-ruffs and the foliage is fine and thread-like, a perfect foil for the silvery-blue straps of the grass* Elymus argentea.

OPPOSITE *Silene or viscaria, clary sage and cornflowers in a harmonious mix of flower colour and size; blends such as this make excellent backdrops to the more clearly defined shapes of perennials.*

ABOVE *In a variety of containers, including plastic cups, seedlings wait to be dealt with; any receptacle will serve the potting purpose as long as it is clean and disinfected. Adequate light is also necessary for sturdy seedling growth, and a covering of silver sand over the surface of the seed-sowing medium keeps moss and algae from growing.*

CENTRE *Outside the greenhouse, the ground lies fallow, waiting for its early spring dressing of well-rotted manure. Inside the greenhouse, the gardener works at her well-ordered bench, pricking out the seedlings which will eventually fill the garden with its annual stock of flowers and vegetables.*

Some hardy annuals can be sown in late summer or early autumn in the places they are to flower, but in spring or early summer they can be sown not only outdoors in situ, but also in pots or trays, along with their half-hardy cousins. They can be pricked out and potted on to make sturdy plants for setting out in mixed border schemes of perennials and shrubs, or else in planting schemes where only annuals are used. By using these pot-grown plants you will find you have a degree more control than you would over plants that are autumn-sown in situ or else self-sown.

If your intention is to plant an entirely annual garden, it would pay to organize your seed-sowing by putting the packets in groups according to colour, and then separate them by height within each colour group. Keep labels handy so that seed is never separated from its name!

Gardening is always said to be a therapeutic pastime. Of all the garden skills, spring seed-sowing is surely the most contemplative. Some might argue that hand-weeding owns this trait, but standing in a warm stillness of the greenhouse on an early spring morning, sifting moist compost into

clean trays, peeling open seed packets, pinching the tiny grains into tidy rows and watering and tagging in an even-paced manner emphasizes the feelings of hope and renewal that lie at the emotional heart of gardening.

Prepare your work area, have sacks of sowing compost ready, and plenty of clean, disinfected seed trays and pots at hand. A soil sieve and a firming tool (made from a piece of wood cut to the size of the trays being used) are also necessary; the soil in a tray must be firmed to help the seedlings develop a strong root system, but not so firm as to compress the compost into a solid block. After filling the trays with compost, breaking up any lumps in process and evening off the surface with a straight edge, simply press the wooden board gently down on the compost surface.

The compost will probably be moist, but this moisture will not be enough to sustain the seed through germination to first true leaves, so water the trays using a fine rose on the watering can. Don't overdo it: you need to moisten the soil, not waterlog it. Adding fungicide to the water will help to prevent damping off.

ABOVE *Among the lushly planted beds of this early-summer garden, annuals and biennials in shades of rose, purple and mauve make a colourful infilling among the more permanent planting of shrubs and perennials. The juvenile plants of some hardy annuals, like pansies, can be set out in their growing positions during the autumn to overwinter, they also serve to provide a modicum of groundcover interest during the barren season and a background to spring-flowering bulbs.*

Seed-sowing is a highly personal technique, and every gardener has his or her own approved method: straight from the packet, tapped gently over its crimped edge; decanted into the palm to be pinched and sprinkled from a low altitude (about 5cm/2in); transferred to a mechanical seed-sower (which rather robs the business of its zen). Find the method that suits you, but aim to sow seed thinly and evenly so that thinning and pricking out are easier to perform.

Water, oxygen, light and an even temperature are the good things all seeds need to grow; too much or too little can be lethal, but that's life, after all. As gardeners we are providers, but with a moderating hand.

Water is absorbed by the seed, which triggers one part of the germination process, swelling the seed to burst its protective coat and so allow more water and oxygen in to further advance the chemical changes of germination.

OPPOSITE *Massed planting in a variety of containers has transformed the sombre façade of a townhouse, creating double borders up the stairs to the front door. Heartsease has been used along with a variety of other violas like the apricot and yellow 'Chantryland', and pansies such as 'Pink Shades' and selections from 'The Sorbet' series. Frequent dead-heading and attention to watering will keep the display looking good for many weeks.*

ABOVE *In early summer, as early spring flowers fade and the perennial plants come more fully into their own, there may be gaps that need filling, and annuals are indispensable for this purpose in every type of garden. Young plants can be dotted among the perennial clumps, or simply grown as individuals in small containers to be positioned around the garden, brightening corners with their clear colours and dainty flowers. Few are as appealing as the simple heartsease (*Viola tricolor*).*

During the days after sowing, and throughout germination and sprouting, careful attention must be paid to keeping the compost moist, never letting it dry out, which would disturb the process and possibly kill the developing plant.

Oxygen is essential to developing seedlings, helping them convert sugar to starch – the foundation of plant growth. It must be present in the soil to be taken up by the plant root hairs, which is why compost must be gently not heavily firmed. Furthermore, oxygen in the soil discourages fungal growth in the compost, helping to ensure seed will not rot before germinating, or damp off once it has.

Light is one of the signals a seed will read to decide if conditions are favourable for successful germination. So, although we are directed to cover seed with compost or to place the tray in a shaded spot, we must be sure not to exclude all light; darkness would just encourage the seed to become dormant (when it 'sleeps' waiting for conditions to

ABOVE Lobelia *'String of Pearls'*, Ageratum *'Pinkie'* and Clarkia *'Amethyst Glow' are low-growing annuals with compact habits which make them ideal for use in traditional border and bedding schemes, where a definite shape is required as well as clear colours.*

CENTRE *In a naturalistic garden where grasses and hardy perennials are encouraged to form self-sustaining groups, annuals and biennials with more open and relaxed shapes and subtle colouring can be encouraged to self-sow. These include* Digitalis lutea *or the cultivar 'Dwarf Temple Bells' both of which will add loose spikes of soft yellow flowers to the early-summer garden.*

improve), or simply sit there past its sell-by date . . . and some seed can be very short-lived. The smaller and finer the seed, the nearer it must be to light to germinate.

Thus, don't bury seed or put it in the shade to germinate; place it in a bright spot, shaded with white paper or a floating cloche or else in a greenhouse that has been painted with horticultural sunblock. And once the seed is up and sprouting, make sure it has adequate light so that it does not become etiolated.

Temperature is where gardeners most often go wrong – putting trays in spots too cold to allow germination or so

hot that the seed springs to life, swelters and dies. Invest in a thermometer to keep tabs on the ambient temperature on windowsills or in airing cupboards, the favoured alternatives to heated propagating units.

Temperature is even more likely to affect your planning the further north or south you live; many plants can withstand temperatures of −18 to −23°C (0° to −10°F), but in cold northern zones, gardeners must consider hardiness even more critically, and sow and raise hardy annual plants under glass during autumn and winter to bed out in spring. In the south, where winters are considerably warmer, summer hardiness is a consideration. Plants need cool

ABOVE *Combining annuals and biennials with perennials offers all sorts of giddy opportunities to play one plant off against another. The mingling of this brilliant white, heavy-flowered Canterbury bell among the more delicate, tiny-flowered spikes of white valerian emphasizes the character of each plant; white-flowered violas weave their way through the lower stalks and leaves of their upright-growing companions, providing another layer of floral interest.*

LEFT *The informality of a self-sown annual garden is part of its charm, and it is often remarked that Mother Nature is the best, but not the tidiest, gardener. In early summer, volunteers marching in from other parts of the garden, or from nearby meadows and hedges, will find their way into purposely sown beds to make groundcovering drifts. However, in a garden as in life, timely intervention is the watchword and to prevent rampant self-sowers from taking over it is important to thin seedlings in early spring, or else to dead-head regularly to control seed production by either snipping off large seedheads or by cutting back small cluster-flowered plants. Linaria 'Fairy Lights' is a robust cultivar of the common toadflax, and wild camomile* (Matricaria recutita) *is a common daisy-flowered meadow plant with an even more robust character. Both, however, respond to cutting back: the linaria will quickly and vigorously bloom again, and the prolific nature of the camomile will be controlled.*

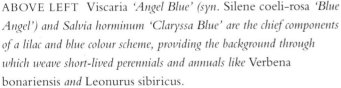

ABOVE LEFT Viscaria *'Angel Blue' (syn.* Silene coeli-rosa *'Blue Angel')* and Salvia horminum *'Claryssa Blue' are the chief components of a lilac and blue colour scheme, providing the background through which weave short-lived perennials and annuals like* Verbena bonariensis *and* Leonurus sibiricus.

ABOVE RIGHT *The idea of creating a one-colour garden is a popular one, but it does demand an understanding of how colour works: that blue is not just blue, but that there are tints, some of which veer towards the red part of the colour spectrum becoming increasingly violet-purple, as in the combination of two plants like the baby-blue* Echium *'Blue Bedder' and the fuchsia-pink* Viscaria *'Angel Rose' (syn.* Silene coeli-rosa *'Rose Angel') , or towars yellow so that the blue takes on an acid-green tinge. When developing a scheme based on colour harmonies, confine the plant choice to flowers that are within the same part of the spectrum.*

night-time conditions to slow their growth so that they do not exceed the energy provided by food made and stored during the day. Care must be taken to sow early enough to ensure plants are ready to put out before summer night temperatures begin to rise.

DESIGNING WITH COLOUR

Colour defines our gardens; by looking at the changing tints of leaf, bark and flower we are able to mark the seasons even in the most subtle of climates. But within each season, too, the colours reflect the phase the garden is passing through – especially in summer, when in the early weeks the predominant colours are opalescent blues, delicate mauves and pinks, shining white and frothy yellow. As the season matures so do the colours, moving to vibrancy and fading to mellow tints.

It has been the fate of annuals to be always associated with the brightest and most in-your-face colour scheming.

ABOVE *Harmonies can be heightened by including touches of the complementary colour, which in the case of blue-purple is yellow-orange. So in this section of border, where there is plenty of blue from* Gilia capitata, *touches of yellow and orange are introduced with random sowings of* Linaria *'Crown Jewels'; orache (*Atriplex hortensis *var.* rubra) *is the purple foliage setting off the brightness of the flower colour.*

This is a legacy of their role in bedding schemes and a perception that was enshrined in the words of William Robinson, written in *The English Garden*, 1883: 'When the bedding system first came into vogue, it was no doubt its extreme brightness, or what we should now call its "gaudiness", that caused it to hold the position it did; but it was soon done to death . . . the constant repetition of this scarlet, yellow, and blue, nauseating even those with little taste in gardening matters, whilst those with finer perceptions began to inquire for the Parsley bed, by way of relief.'

Contrasting colour was *de rigeur* for several generations of garden-makers (and remains so for some to this day), but with the pendulum of fashion in garden design swinging towards the naturalistic style of planting, and a holistic trend to sowing and growing, harmony is the password in colour planning for contemporary gardens.

At the risk of belabouring a point, this trend is not new, and most gardeners today will have been effectively catechized by Gertrude Jekyll's *Colour in the Flower Garden*. Further communion with her works will discover that colour harmony was her dogma. In *Annuals and Biennials*, Miss Jekyll begins the fifth chapter, devoted to colour, thus: 'What is meant by colour schemes is not merely the putting together of flowers that look well side by side, but the disposition of the plants in complete borders in such a manner that the whole effect together is pictorial. It is done by means of progressive harmonies.' An accompanying foldout plan demonstrates her theory, in this instance beginning the border at one end with shades of blue, mauve and white from annuals like love-in-the-mist, cornflowers, nemesia and phacelia, moving on through yellow snapdragons and

limnanthes into orange poppies, crimson hollyhocks, scarlet linaria, pink clarkia, lilac-blue Chinese asters, and pale purple larkspur. White-flowered cosmos, snapdragons, alyssum, sweet peas and phlox are dotted throughout to help the colours blend visually.

In the Jekyll plan, each colour is planted in long irregular swathes rather than blocks, which would further help the eye to blend the colours because you would view the background colours against or through those in the foreground. The temptation with annuals is, I suppose, to plant them in lines or regular shapes, and, of course, sowing the seed in situ requires that it be done in a regular pattern just to enable

OPPOSITE *Candytuft is an old cottage-garden favourite; a bit of a workhorse actually, called upon for edging, for carpet-bedding and similar formal schemes where a long flowering season, strong colours and equally strong, well-defined shape are desirable characteristics. But these qualities are also an advantage to a flowering annual incorporated into a naturalistic or informal plant grouping, like this mixed annual and perennial group. The candytuft cultivar 'Flash Mixed' qualifies on all these counts, so that it sits nicely among the bold foliage of the purple-leaved plantain and the lacy grey-leaved artemisia, popularly known – and quite justifiably so – as 'old warrior' as it is singularly invasive and once it gets a foothold becomes hard to dislodge.*

ABOVE *Another strong grower, but in a different sense, is the wild Pyrenean cranesbill (*Geranium pyrenaicum*), which is strictly speaking a perennial, but self-sows so passionately that it can be treated like a hardy annual. The geranium is not a dense plant, and its sprawling habit creates an openwork colour ground on which to paint a millefleurs tapestry by planting into its network of stems a selection of perennials – oriental poppies, aquilegias, lupins, bearded irises and alliums – like random brushstrokes against the rosy-mauve geranium flowers.*

you to distinguish the weeds from your emerging annual garden. There are a number of ways around this, however, besides following the Jekyll-amoeba pattern. When setting out young plants, you can obtain a random grouping by tossing a handful of pebbles onto the bed and putting a plant where each pebble falls, rather like scattering bulbs to achieve a naturalized effect in grass (be sure to leave adequate space between the plants so that they do not crowd each other out). With seed-sowing, a favourite old-fashioned method described by Mrs Loudon in her *Gardening for Ladies* is to press a plate into the finely raked tilth, making a sowing circle; scatter a few seeds on the firmed ground and then cover over with a dusting of sieved compost.

Mrs Loudon's floral circles are an interesting approach to the problem of achieving a relaxed planting arrangement, and one I imagine works quite well if due care and attention is paid to grading height, varying texture and blending colour in the plants that are sown in the interlocking circles. It would overcome the rigidity that is so often the effect created by sowing annual seed in linear drills.

LEFT *Foxgloves are the quintessential early-summer ephemeral. The graceful, upright spikes laden with pastel bells make perfect companions to lax, spreading bushes of old-fashioned roses. In my own garden I encourage the common pink and white* Digitalis purpurea *to naturalize in the orchard, but among the roses I like to use species such as* Digitalis parviflora, D. lanata *and* D. × mertonensis *or some of the new hybrids of* D. purpurea.

For example, the trellis around a small terrace is wreathed in the roses 'Easlea's Golden Rambler' and 'Pompon de Paris', and bushes of 'Celestial' and 'La Reine Victoria' occupy the borders. The roses are underplanted with low mound-forming cottage-garden perennials like hardy geraniums, lady's mantle and golden marjoram, among which I have dotted the foxglove D. purpurea *'Sutton's Apricot', its peachy-pink tones an excellent foil to the pale pastels of the roses and the upright habit making a strong vertical accent.*

This requires forward planning: foxgloves are biennial and although they will reliably seed themselves, to ensure an annual display it is just as well to use plants raised from spring-sown seed. These can be planted out in early autumn to flower the following season.

TOP RIGHT *The interplay of contrasting textures and shapes in a planting scheme offers just as many intriguing possibilities as the most patiently devised colour plan. Here, a blue foam of tiny globular flowerheads from* Gilia capitata *engulfs the broad leaves of ruby plantain (*Plantago major *'Rubrifolia') beneath a layer of upright-growing* Phacelia tanacetifolia, *which is especially eye-catching for its curious curled flowerheads and finely cut leaf structure. The bright yellow faces of a little viola, haloed in complementary purple, is the colour point that gives depth to the whole grouping.*

CENTRE RIGHT *Foliage is always important in garden design; it is present in the garden much longer than flowers and should always be factored into your plant selections. There are a number of popular flowering annuals whose foliage goes unsung; love-in-the-mist (*Nigella damascena*) for example. Here its finely cut, thread-like leaves knit together behind the starry flowers and offset the blooms of neighbouring plants, including* Viola tricolor, *which is commonly called Johnny jump-ups as it always seems to pop up in the most unexpected places, even when you don't recall sowing the seed!*

BELOW RIGHT *Strong verticals are an important element of garden design, and can be used wherever a moment of drama is needed or you wish to draw the eye to some section of the design. Foxgloves are undoubtedly the best, and certainly the most prevalent, vertical plant in the early-summer garden. In wild or natural gardens, foxgloves seed themselves among mixed tree and shrub plantings, preferring the sunny edge to deep shade. In the formal plan, where space is confined within small box-edged beds, the juxtaposition of scale presented by the foxgloves spires can be especially dramatic.*

OPPOSITE *Fastigiate trees, climbers trained up obelisks and other large-scale verticals come immediately to mind to create height, but even in the context of an annual planting, verticals can be included to prevent the scheme from becoming too predictable. From a foundation of* Malope trifida *'Pink Queen' and 'Vulcan', a pink delphinium spike rises; as the year progresses, it will, in its turn, be replaced by a pink-flowered hollyhock. So the garden is layered in planting and in time.*

RIGHT *At the end of the day, the soft,
smudgy colours that signal the opening weeks
of summer have the most soothing effect.
Among annual flowers, the raspberry tints of
pansies like 'Pink Shades', the washed-out
rose tones of the sweetly fragrant stocks such
as double-flowered 'Appleblossom', and the
innocent blue of love-in-the-mist are easy on
the eye. The undemanding colours of early-
flowering annuals bring to mind a gathering
of well-behaved children at a birthday garden-
party. As the summer proceeds, the party will
become more lively, the flowers bolder and the
colour more demanding of attention, until
eventually the guests begin to tire, their party
gaiety subsides and the garden sinks back into
sedate quietude to wait out the winter.*

*In this restful corner of a little walled
garden, the formal box-edged beds are
carpeted with deep pastel-tinted pansies and
purple linaria and standards of the tender
daisy-flowered marguerite* (Chrysanthemum
frutescens) *are underplanted with luxuriant
sprays of richly fragrant stocks. Their crushed
strawberry colour picks up the pink-tipped
foliage of the* Actinidia kolomitka *trained
on the wall. The harmonious blending of
colours, the fragrance of the flowers trapped by
the surrounding brick walls and the formal
plan combine to give a feeling of tranquillity.*

ABOVE LEFT *The single dusky pink* Rosa mutabilis *is one of the most graceful flowers in the garden, here perfectly complemented by the simplicity of old-fashioned Canterbury bells (*Campanula medium*).*

ABOVE RIGHT *Many annuals have unusually tinted bicolour flowers, including this elegant larkspur, 'Frosted Skies'; this is also a good cut flower and will hold its colour when dried for flower arranging.*

OPPOSITE Lupinus hartwegii *ssp.* cruickshankii *and the cultivar 'Sunrise' are strikingly coloured annual lupins; the fresh colours blend well with early-summer roses and the muted tints of the flowers of other annuals.*

THE SOFT COLOURS OF THE SEASON

Canterbury bells (*Campanula medium*) are among the best of the hardy biennials for late-spring and early-summer display. The upright stems can reach 90cm (3ft), and the bells are white, pink or purple. The Cup-and-Saucer form takes its name from the doubling effect of the petals, which appear to form a rim around the flower. Though these have curiosity value (which may be why they were so popular in old cottage gardens, where novelty was at a premium), the single-flowered sorts are more elegant, and are especially useful for filling-in among roses and low-growing perennials.

Sow the seed in the spring after frost, and prick out into a prepared seedbed in a sheltered part of the garden. The pretty green clumping rosettes can then be moved to their flowering spots in autumn. Try growing a couple of plants in pots to hold as reserves for gap-filling during summer.

Perennial delphiniums are classic border plants, but the hardy annual rocket larkspur (*Consolida ajacis*) is more delicate in its upright habit and panicles of open flower spikes. There are several sorts to choose from for height and flower density. 'Frosted Skies' has the prettiest semi-double white flowers with each petal rimmed in soft china-blue; it grows only to about 45cm (18in) so would work in neatly with other low-growing annuals like love-in-the-mist and some of the annual grasses. Larkspurs should also be grown for cutting and are excellent for dried flower arranging.

Silene sparkles as a shimmering background to love-in-the-mist and the charming species lupin *Lupinus hartwegii* var. *cruickshankii*. The lupin cultivar 'Sunrise' is especially desirable for its crimson and azure-blue flowers which become butter-cream and blue in the uppermost tier of each flower stem. The flowers are also delightfully fragrant and the foliage is an attractive blue-green. William Robinson, in his book *The English Garden*, praised annual lupins as being 'among the most beautiful of hardy annuals, extremely varied in colour and of the simplest culture'. 'Sunrise' must be sown in its eventual flowering position for success, but since the seed is large and germinates readily this is not difficult to achieve.

Among other blue-flowered annuals you could use in the early-summer border, two of my favourites are the

gentian-blue California bluebell (*Phacelia campanularia*) and sky-blue *Gilia capitata*. It is worth noting that they are easy to grow from seed sown in the autumn or spring in their flowering positions, in sun or light shade. Bees love these flowers, and are, in fact, drawn to blue flowers generally, as this is the part of the colour spectrum most visible to bees.

Another bee favourite, and one with particularly striking colour, equalled perhaps only by that of the 'Sunrise' lupin, is the hardy annual *Cerinthe major* 'Purpurascens'. In recent years this has become quite a fashionable plant. It will self-sow quite happily, and from late spring through

summer stretches out its sprawling stems. These are sheathed in glaucous blue-green foliage, which at the flowering tips turn to denim-blue bracts surrounding the dark grape purple tubular flowers – very subtle colouring and very voguish.

INDISPENSABLE ANNUALS

Of all the trailing annuals, lobelia is probably the most popular, but it could never be accused of being fashionable. Hardly a windowbox or container seems to be without an overspill of its flowers in shades of blue, purple, pink, rose or white. The cultivar 'Cascade Mixed' seems to combine all these shades in one blend with the tiny white eye of each flower winking back brightly against a background of burgundy-red, deep violet, pale rosy lilac and rich blue. There is also 'Regatta Blue Splash' with white flowers stained by soft violet-blue; mix this in with the glorious blue-flowered 'Sapphire' and a silver-leaf foliage plant like *Helichrysum petiolaris* for a long-lasting hanging-basket display.

Lobelia are half-hardy annuals so must be sown in gentle heat under glass in the spring. They prefer free-draining situations, so are well-suited to container conditions. To keep them looking at their best, lobelia must be regularly dead-headed, although I've found that rather than attempt to pick off each faded flower individually it is possible to give the plants a light trim by clipping over the flowering stems with kitchen scissors.

Apart from the trailing lobelia, there is also a compact bunching variety that was enormously popular for edging in carpet-bedding schemes. In fact, it still is wherever this type of floral display is maintained. Usually it can be seen planted as ribbons of vividly juxtaposed dark and light colours, which, although eye-catching, is perhaps more suited to public amenity planting than the tasteful confines of your own garden.

Trailing petunias are choice hanging-basket plants, and the sort 'Super Cascade Improved' is an F1 hybrid of some distinction. The colours are a perfect blend with the cascading lobelia mentioned above; the contrast between the little lobelia flowers and the soft silky trumpets of the petunia is most alluring, as is the latter's honeyed scent. One of the clearest memories of my childhood in Midwest America is plucking a petunia blossom to taste the few drops of sweet nectar that collect in the base of each trumpet. I instantly understood why the humming birds paid such close attention to my mother's windowbox garden.

Similarly, the eager upturned faces of the California poppy (*Eschscholzia californica*) always reminds of hot Midwestern summers, so it was, of course, among the annuals I included in my first English garden. Few flowers so completely expunge the memory of damp, chill winter as a bank of golden eschscholzia; even the creamy-coloured sorts have a warming brilliance. However, 'Apricot

LEFT *Trailing lobelia deserves its universal popularity. Few plants flower as freely over as long a period, so it is invaluable as a blender and background plant among more permanent plant groups.*

RIGHT *California poppies and sweet sultan flowers (*Centaurea moschata*) are embedded in the thread-like foliage of fennel against a soft grey ground of* Anaphalis triplinervis.

Flambeau' and 'Inferno' will really raise the temperature. The former has crimped yellow petals splashed with orange; the latter is stirringly scarlet. 'Mission Bells Mixed' has double flowers tinted white, cream, pink and orange.

These poppies will seed themselves, and if first sowings are made in the autumn rather than spring, the plants will be well established in time to provide a fantastic show that begins in early summer. *Eschscholzia* makes a good companion to copper-coloured grasses like *Carex flagellifera* or *C. buchananii*.

Ancient Greek myths recall that as the Mother Goddess, Demeter, wandered the earth searching for Persephone (the daughter abducted by Pluto and carried off to the Underworld), her anguished sorrow was relieved by tasting the bitter liquid seeping from the seedpods of the poppies she had gathered. The medicinal and nutritional values of the opium poppy (*Papaver somniferum*), were well known to most ancient civilizations, just as modern culture is only too aware of the death-dealing danger of its abuse. John Gerard, in his *Grete Herball*, wrote that although the physic

produced from the poppy was invaluable for the relief of all kinds of pain, 'it leaveth behinde it oftentimes a mischiefe worse than the disease it selfe, and that hard to be cured…'. During Victorian times the opium was blended with spirits to make laudanum, just one of many commonly used patent medicines that were based upon this stupefying drug.

It is best to sow the seed where it is to flower, usually in the autumn, as opium poppies don't like to be disturbed by transplanting. In a corner of my garden devoted to pink and rosy-tinted flowers there are usually a few decadent double opium poppies casting a spell along with the slippery petals of their shattered blooms (each flower seems to last only the briefest moment). So it was with some amusement that I read Gertrude Jekyll's warning about giving these annuals a place of their own in the garden: 'If it is convenient to give them a place, autumn sown, away from other plants, it is better to do so, as it has been observed that when they are grown in mixed borders they appear to have a baneful influence on the perennials near them.'

LEFT The genus Papaver *is enormously popular with gardeners, offering 40 or so species, perennial, annual and biennial, from which to choose. Among the annuals there are mop-flowered doubles, uncomplicated single-flowered opium poppies and pompon-doubles such as* P. laciniatum *and* P. paeoniflorum.

*RIGHT The poppy 'Black Peony', shown here growing with dark 'Queen of Night' tulips and drumstick alliums (*A. sphaerocephalon*), is especially desirable for the inky dark depths of the flowers against the soft dove-grey foliage.*

RIGHT *Once upon a time, farm fields were*
bright not only with the blue cornflowers
(Centaurea cyanus) *shown here, but also*
with magenta corncockles (Agrostemma
githago), *yellow corn marigold*
(Chrysanthemum segetum), *and all the*
other wildlings with 'corn' in their names.
The idea of sowing a meadow garden appeals
to romantics, but be warned: to achieve the
real thing requires some intensive gardening.

If you are seeding the meadow, it is essential
to first obliterate all existing vegetation, as most
annual wildflowers are not vigorous enough to
compete with perennial weeds and grasses. Use
a translocating herbicide that travels through
leaves and stems into roots but will not pollute
the soil. If chemical controls are anathema to
you, cut off the light source to deprive the plants
of food by smothering the ground in thick
layers of newspaper, which will decompose and
can be dug in. When the ground is clean, fork
it over and rake down to a fine tilth. Sow a
specially prepared wildflower mix which should
include the fine grasses for a meadowgrass
matrix. Mixes are available in various
combinations for specific soil and site.

Mow the meadow in late summer after the
flowers have shed their seed. Rake the hay up
into sweet-smelling piles to be removed and
composted. Keep a watchful eye for perennial
weeds and dig out any that appear.

Unless you take care to plant a follow-up annual or perennial flower, these poppies are best given a spot in some wilderness or rough area of ground rather than the border proper. This is simply because the flowers go over so quickly, and the withering foliage and stems contribute little as each plant fades. However, the seedheads are good for cutting and drying, so a row sown in the cutting garden would be appropriate.

Some poppies have a black blotch at the base of each petal. 'Daneborg Laced' is a total contrast to this, with a bold pure white splodge on each petal, which is finished off with a lipstick-red fringed and broken edge. This particular poppy is a hardy annual.

Other poppy species worth a place in the garden include the Iceland poppies (*P. nudicaule)*, which are hardy biennials to sow in summer in warm soil in situ, or else in trays for planting out in autumn. The cultivar 'Oregon Rainbows' is a mix of papery-petalled flowers in shades of rose, orange, yellow, cream and white, some of the flowers being picotee-edged with white.

The Umbelliferae family is made up of some truly striking individuals that should be in every garden – even if some of them are frowned on as 'weeds'. But then a common definition of a weed is a plant that is growing where it

LEFT *With flower umbels composed of many starry white flowers and finely divided, ferny foliage,* Ammi majus, *commonly called small bishopweed, is typical of the versatile Umbelliferae family.*

RIGHT *Common hedgerow cow parsley is another umbelliferous flower with undeniable charm, but often rejected as a mere weed.*

shouldn't, so if you choose to place the strikingly pretty annuals in this family in your garden they move up flora's social register a notch or two.

To this family belong many common annual culinary herbs like caraway, dill, chervil, parsley, cumin, coriander, and sweet cicely, as well as medicinal ones like the biennial (and poisonous) hemlock and vegetables including celery, angelica and alexanders, which are said to take their name from the Roman Emperor whose soldiers ate its leaves as we do spinach.

Nowadays, I see alexanders growing wild in the hedgerows – it looks a bit like angelica, with coarse, divided leaves and a large round umbel flowerhead – and admire it, along with the perennial cow parsley and Queen Anne's lace. These delicate 'weeds' are now cultivated in the rough grass under our hazelnut walk and do a good job disguising fading daffodil foliage. In the flower garden borders, however, the annual herbs grow among the perennials since their foliage and muted flowers make such a superb foil for the roses, alliums, delphiniums and other cottage perennials.

MIDSUMMER GLORY

Behold the flowers are diverse in stature, in quality, and colour, and smell and virtue, and some are better than others; also, where the gardener hath set them, there they stand, and quarrel not with one another.

John Bunyan
The Pilgrim's Progress

Few gardeners can be persuaded to leave their gardens during the height of the summer, since it's only during this sometimes all too brief window of opportunity that we get to see the full glory of what we have struggled so hard to achieve. Often, it is the image of summer's bright promise that keeps us going during bleak winter; that can make us disbelieve what is so often professed to be of the utmost importance when planning a garden – year-long colour and interest. But standing in the middle of flower gardens that seem to be bursting at the seams with scented roses,

bright snapdragons, glowing marigolds and zinnias, who can be bothered to think of planning for those bleak grey days when it is so much nicer to stay by the fire compiling want lists from the latest seed catalogue?

Annuals and biennials add an element of unpredictability to the garden; hardy annuals especially, as their talent for self-seeding will find them among perennials and shrubs, springing up where you might never think of placing them, but where they always manage to look just right. In my kitchen garden the original sowing of Shirley poppies (made to brighten up the bean rows) has wandered across the paths and through the garden gate, until the flowers now appear wherever the wind has carried the seed and the soil has been open to receive it.

Perennials are the tried and true, steadfast friends of the summer garden, and unless conditions have been dire or they are planted where soil and site are inappropriate to their needs, they will flower year after year; the clumps may increase in size, but the flower and colours remain virtually unchanged. But sow annuals through the border and suddenly the image changes: gaps between plants fill up

with foliage and the sculptural shapes of some young plants, like biennial verbascum, add texture and form to an otherwise uniform mass of perennial leaf and bloom. Also, in a mixed border or when a planting is looking slightly too predictable to be interesting, a sculptural plant, one with a clearly defined personality, can lift the whole scheme into the realms of quite daring.

Mostly we think of annuals as hugging the ground, or at least never rising much more than knee-height above it. However, there are number of statuesque annuals and biennials from which to select a few show-stoppers. These include members of the verbascum genus, the boldest being *Verbascum olympicum*, and the thistles, which

ABOVE *The soft green discs of trailing nasturtium leaves make a pleasing groundcover throughout mid- and late summer.*

RIGHT *Some biennials, like* Verbascum olympicum, *have an almost sculptural quality. In the first season, their platter-sized leaf rosettes make a weed-smothering mat; in the second season, as the flower spike forms and begins its upward climb, the shape is transformed and the leafy pyramid, seen here amidst a fuzz of* Geranium pyrenaicum *and aquilegias, makes a focal point.*

PREVIOUS PAGE *In my ornamental potager, Shirley poppies have become naturalized, making that part of the garden a more attractive and interesting place to visit while the leafy vegetables are still developing, or filling gaps left by early crops like broad beans. Many other annual flowers, such as pot marigolds (*Calendula officinalis*), tobacco plants (*Nicotiana spp.*) and nasturtiums (*Tropaeolum majus*) will naturalize to serve a decorative and also functional purpose.*

include the legendary Miss Wilmott's ghost (*Eryngium giganteum*) and the towering Scotch thistle (*Onopordum acanthium*).

The verbascum is the most startling to watch in growth, and, since it will seed itself just about anywhere, that is a very easy thing to do. It begins as just a pair of finger-length, grey-felted leaves, but in its first year (it is a biennial or short-lived perennial) it will grow into a huge rosette anchored firmly in place by a long tap root, an indication of its eventual height of 2.5m (8ft). The following year it sends out branches covered in bright yellow flowers that last most of the summer.

The story behind Miss Wilmott's ghost recalls the Edwardian lady gardener Ellen Wilmott and her habit of carrying seeds of eryngium in her pocket; when visiting a garden she would surreptitiously scatter a pinch in a likely spot. The next year, up would pop this bleached silvery-green thistle, each flowerhead grasped by a broad, spiky collar like some pugnacious floral bulldog: by all accounts, Miss Wilmott was herself a bit of a handful. In spite of its species name, it is, at 1.2m (4ft), only half the height of its Scotch thistle cousin. The latter has the same silvery-grey colouring, but the foliage is less glossy than that of Miss Wilmott's Ghost. When the prickly, branching flower stalks and leaves reach full girth it is one mean plant, so site it thoughtfully. And keep an eye on the flowerheads – they seed with gay abandon. This trait is shared by its cousin, *Silybum marianum*, commonly called Blessed Mary's thistle. Every year, at summer's end, I regret the day I introduced this plant to my garden: I watch the seedheads form and

stand ready, secateurs in hand and industrial gauge gauntlets nearby, to dash out to cut them down before the downy seed scatters to the four winds. But each spring, as I spot the vast spreading rosettes of dark green foliage netted in silvery-white veins take shape, I stand back and admire the stunning achievement of that single seed which escaped my autumn putsch. We gardeners are a contrary bunch.

Using large-format annuals as dot plants in an informal mixed border planting is a step on from their use in the old-fashioned formal bedded-out sort of garden. Planting

LEFT *Beneath the wiry stems of* Verbena bonariensis *a rich mix of annual and perennial flowers fill an informal border;* Viscaria *'Angel Rose' (syn.* Silene coeli-rosa *'Rose Angel'),* Echium *'Blue Bedder' and the blue flax* Linum perenne *have the saturated colouring that characterizes the midsummer garden.*

ABOVE *The French marigold* Tagetes *'Golden Gem' grows into flower-covered mounds and makes a firm outline for more formal layouts as in the kitchen garden, between rows of lettuce and dwarf French beans.*

annuals in drifts was also quite a popular technique, and it is a bit more exciting to think about doing this using only annuals with striking foliage; for example a mid-border ribbon of maroon-coloured *Perilla frutescens*, or dwarf *Euphorbia marginata* 'Summer Icicle', which, as you might guess from the name, has green leaves margined with white.

In the previous chapter I mentioned Gertrude Jekyll's plan for a double border of annuals, organized according to drifts of colour. There are some annuals and biennials which, as well as having fine colour, also have an open, airy form or slender, upright shape that makes them ideal for intermingling with perennials. They usually grow from tight basal rosettes that won't take up much ground space between the perennials.

As the flecks of annual colour speckle the background behind a group of clearly defined perennial flowers, the annual blooms help to blend the bolder flowers into a pleasing visual whole in the same way that a painter might use tiny brush strokes of some intermediate or complementary tint to unite the main elements of a composition. By

midsummer, the flower colours of perennials, annuals and biennials are becoming more intense and if you're going for the drift effect it might be a good idea to use some of the annual blenders to help the colour combinations along; without some intermediary tints the contrasts between saturated colours might be too jarring.

Venus navelwort (*Omphalodes linifolia*) and annual baby's breath (*Gysophila elegans*) are both white, small-flowered, medium-height plants that would work well among blues and pale lilacs; *Smyrnium perfoliatum* and *Nicotiana langsdorffii* both have the yellow-green flowers that blend so well

LEFT *The giant flower spikes of Turkey sage (*Salvia sclarea *var.* turkestanica) *need plenty of space, and a broad swathe of this biennial has a dramatic impact (as does the scent, which is somewhat foxy, but not unpleasant). The muted lavender-blue and white flowers are an excellent contrast among the warmer colours of this border.*

RIGHT *A vivid mix of yellows from* Anthemis arabica *'Criss-Cross' and* Chrysanthemum carinatum *'Primrose Gem' and white-petalled 'Monarch Court Jesters' is set off by the apple-green 'flowers' of the half-hardy annual bells of Ireland (*Moluccella laevis)*, a long-lasting cut flower which is good for drying.*

certainly focuses the mind on the beauty of single (as opposed to pompon double) hollyhocks. It also gives rise to the idea of sowing broad drifts of hollyhocks along a stretch of path through the garden – that would be show-stopping!

The placement of annuals and biennials in the garden follows many of the same principles as arranging perennial plants. It used to be that there were 'rules', the most stringent being that tall plants go at the back, medium plants in the centre and small plants at the front. This has been relaxed in many modern gardens, and with annuals it is especially easy to let go of the precepts when you allow them to find their own home by self-seeding. So pull the tall verticals to the front, jumble up the medium-height branching sorts with the sprawling stragglers, and tip-in the clump-forming tinies to create movement and avoid the static nature of a conventional annual planting.

However, one aspect of planting will always remain true: the plants must have enough room to develop properly, so take care to thin seedlings adequately to allow each individual the light and shade necessary for steady, sturdy

among orange and red plants. Alternatively, encourage *Schizanthus pinnatus* to scatter its bee-shaped, purple flowers with yellow throats and make a bridge between those complementary colours.

One of the most impressive drift gardens I have ever seen is, like so many good features, the result of happy accident and vigorous self-seeding. In a small village lane, hollyhocks of every colour have placed themselves all along the edge of the path. It is sensational to walk along this lane, and it

LEFT *In the second season, the stubby flower stem of the biennial silver sage (*Salvia argentea*) emerges with the same silvery fur coat as its leaves (see below), eventually developing into a many-branched candelabra of pale white flowers. Plants with this much character are definitely ones to be showcased.*

RIGHT *Using biennials in the mixed border requires forward planning, and patience, too. Although the flowers are not present during the first season, biennials like the silver sage are worth waiting for. Even in its first year, this plant makes a striking rosette of big, broad, heavily felted leaves which are so pale and silvery as to be nearly white.*

LEFT Atriplex hortensis *var.* rubra, *commonly known as red orache, is one of the best foliage annuals, and is completely at home in the informal garden where the dark beetroot-red colour of its leaves and stems makes a pleasing backdrop to the warm tones of midsummer perennials, like the pink-flowered bergamot* Monarda 'Beauty of Cobham', Veronicastrum virginicum 'Inspiration' *and* Verbena hastata 'Rosea'. *Also, orache has the strong vertical growth habit that is so useful in plantings designed for drawing the eye towards certain features by either creating harmonies or contrasts of shape. This pronounced verticality persists over a long period, as does the colour interest; as the curious flower-plume turns to seed, the foliage turns crimson-orange, eventually taking second place to the ripening seeds that become clusters of warm biscuit-brown as the season draws to a close. Strong outlines, as presented by the dark mass of the orache, will also give substance to a loose, unstructured blend of perennial flowers.*

growth. No matter how hard it hurts to uproot all those promising seedlings, do it, because it is even more painful to watch an etiolated youngster, pale and wan, struggle to get a foothold in the garden, and then ultimately succumb to disease.

Follow the same rule when planting out; allow enough space for basal leaves to develop without overlapping or smothering neighbouring plants. In the case of a plant such as *Salvia argentea* (shown on pages 60–1), this can mean as much as 30cm (12in) between plants, but the thick grey-felted leaves soon spread out to smother weeds (which is allowed) and the following season send up the broad branching candelabra flower stalk which itself needs plenty of room around it to really show off its beauty.

For some of us containers provide the only garden-making space that we can enjoy. Apartment-dwellers with compact terraces or amenable windowsills, townhouse residents with walled courtyards, and rooftop gardeners face the greatest challenge in exercising their ingenuity to raise a wide range of flowering plants in often hostile conditions. Because, let's face it, containers are confining: the soil dries out quickly, nutrients leach out with the frequent watering required, the situation is often exposed, and aphids can even find their way to the 38th floor.

There are formal container gardens and informal ones. An informal sort would be one which is an amalgam of diverse pots, baskets and boxes planted with annuals in a wide range of colour and shape, the only unifying factor being the gardener's desire to garden. One of the best formal container gardens I know is on a rooftop in the heart of

downtown Manhattan; the formality comes from the colour scheme, which is restricted to black, white and silver-grey. The sizeable pots have all been painted with matte black paint and permanently planted with shrubs or small trees. Each summer they are also filled with annuals purchased from the flower markets of New York City, using a range of trailing variegated foliage plants and white-flowered annuals.

In the not so distant past it seemed that it was only possible to buy annuals in a limited range of colours and

few seed trays on a warm windowsill may be adequate to provide a few plants, if you need them in any number I suggest a trip to the local garden centre or nursery where you can stock up on 'rent-a-crowd' flowers to fill windowboxes, baskets and all the other containers you are able to gather together.

When making your selections, look for plants that are strong-growing, with healthy, clean foliage. Check for roots growing from the bottom of the pots or trays; if roots are growing through, the plants have been in the trays too long and will be slow to take off after transplanting. You may be drawn to select the trays covered with the most flowers. This is not necessarily a good thing, and may be sign of stress, with the plants desperately flowering in the rush to set seed and die, which is what they are genetically programmed to do. Well-greened sturdy foliage is more likely to indicate a good plant; they will flower soon enough provided you don't set them out too early. Be sure all danger of frost is past – containers may receive some protection from walls and city microclimates, but why risk it? The plants will establish quickly as the weather warms and you begin the life-sustaining routine of feeding and watering.

varieties, but nurserymen and other suppliers have woken to the fact that we gardeners are a tasteful crowd, and they are now providing ready-to-plant stock in a range of individual and interesting colours so that we can scheme to our hearts' content using pre-packs of ready-sorted colour-themed annuals, or picking and mixing our own.

Seed merchants, too, have taken to providing collections of annual seed sorted by colour. But if you live in a situation where your garden space is severely restricted, chances are the growing area will be, too, and although a

ABOVE *Windowboxes are most frequently the domain of hardy and half-hardy annuals; garden centres and nurseries are awash each spring with 'summer bedding'. Lavish displays have their place, but so do quiet groups of annuals, like this 'monoculture' of a dwarf form of tobacco plant with cherry-red flowers. Grown in a few terracotta pots, the relaxed arrangement complements the tubful of half-hardy* Heliotropium *'Marine'. Both these plants are fragrant, and pot-growing helps to bring the flowers and scent nearer to appreciative noses.*

ABOVE *The blue and white theme of the perennial planting in the box-edged beds of this garden is carried through into the container planting of dwarf tobacco plant* Nicotiana *'Dwarf White Bedder' and the blue and lilac petunias.*

RIGHT *The* Nicotiana *genus has species and cultivars in a wide variety of shapes and sizes. As well as the dwarf bedders there is the statuesque* Nicotiana sylvestris, *which makes a plant nearly 1.2m (4ft) tall with long, tubular, white flowers. It will naturalize beneath trees and among shrubs; the scent will fill the evening garden.*

THE SCENTED GARDEN

Containers are also an obvious place to grow annuals and biennials for their scent: if the garden is portable, the plants can be positioned to allow the fullest appreciation of their perfume. However, scented annuals and biennials also have a place in the open garden, usually somewhere sheltered so the perfume can be contained and not dispersed instantly on the breeze. Near paths and close to seating are obvious sites to choose.

As Gertrude Jekyll pointed out in her book on annuals, most of the most perfumed flowers in the group belong to the Cruciferae family. This always amuses me, since this is the cabbage family, and the smell of the boiled vegetable may be more familiar than the sweetness of wallflowers, rocket or stocks. The foul-smelling weed tobacco also has some deliciously scented cousins; the smell of *Nicotiana alata* on the evening breeze of a warm summer night is one of life's great joys, while the stately *N. sylvestris* has fine scent and flowerheads made up of long white pendant tubes that flare to the typical star at their tips. It is quite strong-growing, and looks really well in isolated clumps beneath trees or among shrubs. The night-scented stock *Matthiola bicornis* is similarly fragrant, and then there is the night phlox *Zaluzianskya capenensis*, its starry white flowers releasing a powerful fragrance on humid summer evenings.

Daytime perfumes are released by such old-fashioned favourites as sweet pea (especially the dark maroon and lavender-blue 'Matucana', which was supposedly introduced to the UK from Sicily in 1700; seed given to me by a friend from his family's old Tuscan garden produced just such a flower, with a remarkably strong perfume). Snapdragons (*Antirrhinum*) are another old cottage-garden favourite for perfume, as well as mignonette (*Reseda odorata*), which was often grown in pots by Victorian lady gardeners to scent the boudoir. Another old favourite is the incense plant, *Humea elegans*. Vita Sackville-West wrote of it, 'It is neither showy nor conspicuous, and nothing but the scent would lead you to it among its more garish companions . . . yet it is graceful in its growth and well deserves its adjective,

RIGHT *By midsummer, the potential of some annual flowers to contribute structural quality to the planting scheme is being fully realized. As their colour contribution recedes with the falling away of the petals, the seedheads, stems, bracts and growth habits (pendulous, upright, branching and so on) peculiar to each plant are revealed. These in turn help to lengthen the season of a plant's interest, and subsequently the garden's ability to hold our attention.*

As part of a broader border planting, the contrast between the tubby, flagon-shaped seedpods of the opium poppy ensures that they are the perfect complement to the finger-like spikes of the perennial Veronicastrum virginicum album. *Furthermore, as the veronicastrum flower spike turns to seed it blackens, while the poppy becomes faded eau de Nil, so that while the shapes are in contrast the dying tones are in complete harmony. The lesson here is never to be in too much of a hurry to tidy up the garden; some of the terminal colours are just as attractive as the flowers, and infinitely more subtle.*

elegans.' She described growing it as a half-hardy biennial planted out in 'odd corners, where people pass, or sit on benches', but concludes with a caution against its rash-producing potential for people who may be allergic to it.

Sweet william (*Dianthus barbatus*), sweet sultan (*Centaurea moschata*) and sweet rocket or dame's violets (*Hesperis matrionalis*) are just a few more scented annuals and biennials to look for in seed lists.

When I began planting my first garden, I was long on dreams but short on space. It was essentially a courtyard with a pocket of grass tacked on one edge; I named my garden 'Little Ease', but my husband referred to it as the *oubliette*, where much was planted and soon forgotten.

One plant I shall never forget was the single seedling of *Cobaea scandens* donated by a neighbour; 'Give it room to climb,' she counselled. This was easy to do, because in a small space the horizontal plane is quickly filled, leaving up the only way to go. I installed a pergola, some trellis and the cobaea. It went off like a rocket, sending its chubby bell-shaped blossoms up and over the pergola. Commonly called cup and saucers, it originates from Mexico and is really a frost-tender perennial, but it grows so easily from

LEFT *There are several annual climbers that you should try growing, if only for the truly amazing speed with which they will cover a support. One of the quickest, and with quite showy flowers, is* Cobaea scandens, *the cup and saucer plant; the seedheads are also an asset.*

RIGHT *Umbellifer seedheads, in this case those of fennel (*Foeniculum*), have a particularly sympathetic shape for use as accents among other annuals and perennials.*

seed and so prolifically in its first year that you might just as well annualize it. The flowerbuds are white and age to purple, but the cultivar 'Alba' remains a pristine white.

Rhodochiton atrosanguineus is also a frost-tender perennial, and it also makes free with its flowers in the first year. However, its blooms are rather more understated; they are slender deep purple pendant tubes beneath a dusky pink calyx, reminding me of a catwalk model sheltering beneath an umbrella. The heart-shaped foliage is bright green with a similar dusky tinge, and a few plants twining up a delicate wire support can look most exotic.

Supports are critical when using annual climbers; generally they tend to be rather delicate compared to perennial climbers, so the supports should not overwhelm the plant. The vivid blue morning glory (*Ipomoea tricolor*) is a favourite annual climber in cool temperate climates – if you've ever seen it grow in its native subtropical zones you'll know the meaning of breathtaking. Give it a place in full sun without too much competition and provide something delicate to support the stems, such as green tarred garden twine strung vertically between the ground and roof overhang on the sunny side of the house. Train the morning glory up the strings to make a flowering curtain. *Ipomoea alba* is the truly exotic moon flower, so called for its shining white face and nocturnal perfume.

Sweet peas are traditionally supported on netting to provide good blooms for cutting, but if you don't mind sacrificing cut-flower perfection, they will enjoy clambering about in the border. In fact, they will self-sow, although you will wind up with random flower colours. Other

annual plants that can climb up on shrub and perennial shoulders to reach the sun are Chilean glory vine (*Eccremocarpus scaber*), with tubular flowers in shades of red, orange and yellow that last well into the autumn, canary creeper (*Tropaeolum peregrinum*), which has luminous yellow flowers, and *Tropaeolum polyphyllum*, with similar flowers but the further advantage of steely blue-grey foliage.

Vegetables present some unusual annual candidates for the ornamental garden; don't scoff at the humble squash and gourd because there are some charming dwarf strains that are multicoloured, curiously shaped, and sometimes quite baroque in appearance. Train these up and over a pergola and watch as the big yellow flowers turn into collectable little knick-knacks (once the gourds are dried and varnished, of course).

The charm of runnerbeans as a vegetable is questionable as the taste is so uninteresting. The flowers are another matter, however, and the old variety 'Painted Lady' provides the prettiest. Its orange and white bicoloured blooms look very fine gracing an arbour or thatching a pergola; the scent is of delicious honey and I love to pick a bunch for decoration, which is exactly what runner beans were first grown for on their introduction to Europe from Central America in the 16th century.

LEFT AND CENTRE *Sweet peas are among the most loved of annual flowers; the older varieties seem to have the sweetest perfume. They are gross feeders, so need to be sown in deeply dug and heavily manured soil. If you start the seeds in the greenhouse during early spring, with some heat, be sure to use deep pots to give the roots plenty of room to develop; cardboard tubes from paper towels and so on cut to 10cm (4in) lengths are especially good for the purpose. Pack the tubes tightly into a tray so they support each other and then plant directly into the flowering positions after the last frost. The tubes will rot down and the peas will grow away quickly.*

Make sure the peas have good supports; in the border use thin canes tied together to make tripods, or else use twiggy 'peasticks' to make an armature of interwoven branches. This system is most useful when the peas are being grown as a centrepiece in a formal planting scheme. Alternatively, you can let the peas self-sow, which they will do where weather conditions are not too harsh. In time the plants will decrease and eventually die out, but while they persist the natural effect can be extremely pretty.

ABOVE *Half-hardy, pink-tinted,* Phlox drummondii *'Brilliant' and* Nemophila menziesii *'Baby Blue Eyes' in sparkling partnership.*

LEFT *Close-cut grass paths mark the way through a superb example of naturalistic border planting, where annual and perennial flowers, and broad-leaved foliage plants exist in a self-supporting community. The matrix is formed to the exclusion of ornamental grasses except for several specimen clumps of miscanthus. It is mainly the contrasts between the horizontal line of the umbellifer seedheads and the strong verticals of plants like Verbascum chaixii 'Album' that make this blend so entrancing.*

To a degree, this informal planting scheme is also self-sustaining, as many of the plants will seed themselves. From time to time the intervening hand of the gardener is required to thin and redistribute the annual volunteers so that the planting is not overcome by any single particularly gregarious species, such as fennel. Perennial plant skeletons, too, will have to be cut down in the spring and removed to make way for the coming year. But staking, weeding and other on-going garden practices are replaced by the once or twice yearly clear-up and 'management' replaces 'gardening'.

Fennel is a comely umbellifer and a perennial. However, unless large clumps are desired, it is best disciplined as an annual, as young plants have the most grace.

MIDSUMMER TASKS

As summer gets into full swing there will still be plenty of tasks to execute in order to establish vigorous displays of annuals and biennials. One of the most important jobs is thinning. It is worth stressing again that young plants need space to develop properly, and overcrowding leads to disease and wasted effort.

Annuals that were sown in the spring will be well-established by now, and should have been thinned, but it is possible that some seeds were sown later, even into early summer, in order to have flowers in late summer. These will require thinning now, and as summer progresses, the days get warmer and there is less chance of rain, so this must be done with more preparation and care.

Begin by watering the seedlings to be thinned, making sure that the soil is moist, though not sodden. This will make it easier to tease the little plantlets apart from their near neighbours without causing too much disturbance to developing root systems. It will also help to maintain a cool, moist atmosphere around the thinned patch of seedlings so that they should recover quite well from the interference. No matter how careful you are, some disturbance is inevitable.

Pinch out the smallest seedlings, lifting them from the soil by their leaves, spacing the remaining plants according to the recommendations on the seed packet – usually 10–15cm (4-6in) apart. If you have some spare ground elsewhere in the garden, or want to have a reserve planting for cut flowers, conserve the lifted seedlings by keeping their roots moist and their immature little leaves shaded.

As the seedlings are lifted, the soil may become loosened around the remaining plants; firm it gently with your fingertips. Then water the bed again, perhaps adding a fungicide to the water to prevent any chance of damping off.

Take care to water all the plants during the summer, and take care to water evenly and regularly; it is no use to them to have 'feast or famine', as drought conditions will stunt their growth and render them susceptible to disease.

Birds and neighbourhood cats are the next big threat to developing annuals, although some gardeners also have to deal with bigger pests such as deer. Netting stretched over

As the taller-growing annuals begin to gain height, be sure to get any support in place in good time; it is most difficult to stake a fully developed plant discreetly.

Peasticks provide the most natural-looking supports; these are simply twiggy branches cut in the spring before the sap begins to rise. Trim the cut ends of the branches to a point to make it easy to poke them into the flowerbed, and then distribute them around the bed so that the twiggy branchlets criss-cross over the seedlings. As the plants grow, their foliage and flowers will completely disguise the peasticks.

Rigid supports such as bamboo canes or plastic-covered rods and netting will never permit a natural look and should be used only in the cutting garden where plants are being raised in tidy rows. However, it would be an idea to support a massed planting of hollyhocks, or some other tall-growing subject, with a grid made of mesh stretched between secure corner and side supports. The flower stems will grow up and through the mesh which will give them adequate support, so that they won't be knocked sideways by strong winds or heavy rain.

After all this advice, there is one more counsel of perfection: don't forget to feed. All plants benefit from additional nutrients, specifically nitrogen (N) for green growth, phosphate (P) to promote quantity and productivity of flowers, fruit and vegetables, and potash (K) for

the seedlings as they grow, deterrent scent pellets, cat-mobiles with glittering glass marbles for eyes, inflatable barn owls, even plastic pop bottles filled with water and dotted around the border – these are just a few of the tactics gardeners have tried. It is impossible to recommend a method, since what works for one person may have no effect for another. But, generally speaking, it is said that: cats dislike water; glittering, jittering objects deter birds (humming tape is good); moles dislike vibration; and large mammals have trouble with large fences. Deterrent smells can be off-putting to humans too!

ABOVE *Orange* Mimulus luteus *contrasts with the dark reddish-brown of* Plantago major *'Rubrifolia' and red orache in a grouping of rich saturated mid- to late summer colour.*

improving quality of flower, scent and so on. Today's gardeners know this formula as NPK, in earlier days it was called the Golden Tripod, and was described in a gardener's manual from 1933: 'Remove a leg from a tripod and over it falls. Planted firmly on its three legs, a slender tripod is capable of supporting a great weight. If we give our plants a free supply of potash, phosphate and nitrate under healthy conditions they will grow and flower exceedingly and as the season and climate will allow.' Modern fertilizers will have their composition clearly indicated as percentages of NPK, so a balanced fertilizer will have equal amounts, such as 20-20-20. If the final number is higher, potash levels are greater than nitrogen and phosphate.

Phosphates are available in various forms, but of most value to the gardener is superphosphate. Hardy annuals that have overwintered can be given a dressing of this fertilizer to wake them up in early summer and to promote good flowering. Don't overdo it, but follow the manufacturer's instructions, usually expressed as applying so many grammes per square metre or millilitres if applied in solution as a foliar feed. By midsummer's end, when the flowers are beginning to struggle to maintain their show, I give the garden another dose of foliar feed to encourage a new crop of flowers. This is especially important if you've been dead-heading and cutting back, which is one of gardening's most pleasing tasks.

LEFT *In dry conditions or a container, a creamy white zinnia planted among the clary sage* Salvia horminum *'Claryssa' – selected for its white bracts – would make fine companions for plants with cream-variegated leaves or grey foliage such as that of* Ballota acetabulosa.

CENTRE *White-flowered everlastings, helichrysum and statice mingle with mallow blooms in a pleasing mix of shapes and textures.*

RIGHT *Just as Pointilliste painters such as Georges Seurat used small dots of pure colour to render an image, reasoning that tints and values should be blended in the viewer's eye rather on the palette, using small-scale flowers as dots of colour will have the same effect, as the plants are viewed through them; here, cow parsley brings the floral composition together.*

Plants are programmed to propagate: to flower, set seed, and then die. As a flower fades, the growth energy is directed to seed production. Remove the faded flower, and the energy goes into producing another flower in a renewed effort to set seed.

On a warm summer evening, when the breeze is barely stirring and the scent of nicotiana fills the garden, it is exceptionally soothing to scan the flowerbeds, plucking off a faded flower here, snipping a stem with sharp secateurs there. Approach the task systematically, do it cleanly (using flower arranger's scissors will avoid the possibility of tearing the plant from the ground), and always cut the stem back to a leaf joint, where new growth will come from.

LEFT *The earliest gardens were herb and vegetable gardens, where these plants were grown for profit (sale at market), physic (medicine), and potage (food); hence the name potager. And among the familiar herbs and veggies there were many flowers growing, for they also numbered among the ranks of the '3-Ps'.*

As time and fashion moved on, the vegetable and herb garden became divorced from the flower garden, as it was deemed unsuitable to grow smelly cabbages and onions among the sweet flowers that continued to be grown near the house. Thus, the kitchen garden found its way to the outer perimeters of the garden; ostracized by fashion, which in the 18th and 19th centuries regarded the garden purely as a source of visual pleasure and stimulation. And there, in the Old World anyway, we seem to have stuck – the garden as an artifact. New World and naturalistic gardens, however, have broken the mould, bringing together the visual stimulus of an attractive garden scene which is also an active part of living. Begin again with the vegetable garden, scatter flowers among the corn, and make the garden the place you live in. As Thomas Church so famously remarked, 'Gardens are for people.'

THE EDIBLE GARDEN

The vegetable garden has the potential to be the most intriguing part of any garden, and vegetables themselves offer some intriguing opportunities for inventive gardening in beds and borders. As annuals, vegetables present the garden designer with a whole range of leaf size, shape and texture, with colours ranging from dark green to bright pink and purple. And in some cases, if the vegetables are left to flower, the results can surprise you. Chicory is a good example, its sky-blue discs looking wonderful spangled through the dark feathers of bronze fennel foliage.

Joy Larkcom gives some excellent recommendations in her indispensable book *Creative Vegetable Gardening*, in particular the method of mixing carrot seed with annual flowers like flax (*Linum usitatissimum*), cornflowers, godetia,

larkspurs, love-in-the-mist, and other annuals that have light feathery foliage like that of the carrots. She notes that not only do the flowers show off brilliantly against all this fine greenery, but the mix-up has a camouflaging effect, keeping the crop clear of carrot fly. No mean trick! If you decide to use this method, which would work with other root vegetables, the recommended ratio is half flower and half vegetable seed, mixed in a cup and then sown in broad ribbons or patches rather than in tidy rows.

Ornamental vegetable gardens, or potagers, have been popular on and off for centuries; generally the format was one of raised beds separated by neat pathways and edged with boards or brick to maintain the structure of the bed. There are practical advantages to this more obviously aesthetic system: because the soil of the raised beds is never

ABOVE, LEFT TO RIGHT *Annual flowers and vegetables have a natural affinity, combining as well in the kitchen garden as they do on the kitchen range. Many flowers are edible and bring colour and subtle flavour to recipes, others are useful as 'companions' to vegetables repelling or distracting insect pests from crops.*

Formally-arranged potagers most often incorporate flowers among the vegetables; French marigolds and blood-red salvias fill the box-edged central beds of a charmingly traditional farm garden, where the beds are divided by a bark-mulched path.

Stone pavers demarcate the flower- and vegetable-filled beds in a more modern interpretation of the old-style kitchen garden, while a more relaxed approach is adopted by a mixed planting of lettuces spread beneath the spikes of verbascum and leeks which have begun to go to seed, sending up their curiously bulbous blossoms.

walked upon it is looser, which means that it warms earlier and plants can make easier headway putting down roots and so produce more and earlier crops. Soil fertility is also easier to sustain through regular heavy mulchings of well-rotted manure or composted garden waste, and the use of nutrient-rich short-season crops which are sown and then quickly dug into the soil before they turn to flower.

This system, known as green manuring, uses quite a few ornamental annuals, including sunflowers (but only in the small plantlet stage), buckwheat, cowpeas, and the pretty blue *Phacelia tanacetifolia*, which has appeared elsewhere in the book among the flowers of early summer. The latter is especially good as an early-season green manure, to be dug in by early to midsummer to provide a good moisture-retentive soil for winter-cropping vegetables. Winter-cover

crops of crimson clover (*Trifolium incarnatum*) can be sown at the end of summer, to provide a living mulch on fallow beds during winter, and then dug in during early spring. Although using a green manure depends upon digging in the crop before it flowers, a reason can always be found to leave a few clumps to make flowers, as Joy Larkcom points out. Thus, by leaving several strategically placed bunches of phacelia in a bed planted with red cabbages, a decorative colour effect can be achieved from functional beginnings.

There are some fine decorative vegetable annuals, including curly kale (which also makes a fine green manure). It has deep green frazzled leaves that stand in the garden throughout winter like feather dusters atop stout canes. Grown among perennial Michaelmas daisies of medium height, or with grasses like coppery-green *Stipa arundinacea*, it would make a fine contribution to the autumn garden at a time when foliage effects are getting a little short. Similarly, ornamental kales and cabbages have become firm favourites at nurseries and garden centres, nestling among the pumpkins and poinsettas for seasonal decoration. In the flower garden they look most comfortable grown in containers, with winter-flowering pansies in

ABOVE, LEFT TO RIGHT *Colour contrasts and harmonies have a role to play in the vegetable garden: red and white-flowered runner beans twine around the stems of a pale petalled sunflower like 'Italian White'; Echium 'Blue Bedder' attracts bees to the kitchen garden and also highlights the glaucous blueness of brassica foliage; bright green moss-leaved parsley makes a complementary support to the vivid crimson blooms of trailing nasturtium.*

harmonizing shades of purple, pink, cream and white, but in the potager they look terrific marking the intersections of main pathways or as the centrepiece to a formal planting of leeks and red cabbage.

For red tints try out ruby chard; the stems are blood-red and glossy, while the dark green leaves are deeply marked by veins that seem to be flowing with burgundy. There are a number of red lettuces, like 'Lollo Rosso' and 'Red Oakleaf', or radicchio, the Italian red chicory, which is marbled red and creamy white; there are also red brussels sprouts, red perilla or shisho (a Japanese leaf vegetable much

used by Victorian gardeners in bedding-out schemes) and dark purple-red basil varieties, some with curly leaves. The white kernel sweetcorn, like 'Platinum Lady' has dark purple foliage and stalks; there is also a variegated-leaf sweetcorn that is perfect for use in the flower garden as well as the ornamental potager.

Blue among vegetables is not a true blue but rather more steely blue-green, such as you find in the leaves of leeks and some of the autumn and winter cabbages. Sometimes these veggies take on a silvery sheen which makes a fetching backdrop for darker greens. Yellow you can find in yellow-stemmed chard, but I don't know that you can count yellow tomatoes or yellow fruiting courgettes, since in my garden at least they are never long on the vine before they've disappeared into the kitchen.

Using these multicoloured vegetables as foliage backdrops to the potager, you can stir in annual flowers to paint the most elaborate pictures. And if you want to be totally in tune with the ecological ethic of organic gardening, you can use the flowers as companion plants, combining flowers, herbs and vegetables that are mutually beneficial, either

LEFT *Incorporating vegetables into a bedding scheme opens up whole new realms of foliage interest. Brassicas offer some of the best-quality leaves, as here, where red cabbages shape the planting of a rondel at the centre of a formal drive. In the low light of a summer afternoon, the curious purple tinge and rounded shape of the cabbage leaves are accented by the various neighbouring annuals and perennials.*

RIGHT *Some vegetables are at their best when they bolt, for example this ornamental kale, showing-off frilled margins and coloured ribs and leaf veins.*

because they help each other to grow healthily because they possess some substance that the other needs, or because they have insect- or disease-repelling properties.

Probably the best known companion flowers are the French marigolds (*Tagetes*), valued for dealing with soil nematode infestations, but only if they are grown for several seasons in the same spot. However, planting them among tomatoes is said to increase crop yields. Another old favourite is garlic planted beneath roses to repel aphids; larkspurs are said to have the same property. Nasturtiums help squash come into fruit more quickly and will repel aphids of all kinds (grow the climbing sort through apple trees to ward off woolly aphids, and beneath cabbages and with potatoes to the benefit of the vegetable crop).

Not all beneficial annuals are ornamental, and indeed one of the most desirable from a companion planting point of view is also one of the most tenacious 'weeds' in our gardens: the unconquerable pig weed or lamb's quarters (*Chenopodium album*). Here is a plant that has been with us ever since Adam and Eve first messed about in their garden; it has a global presence and for every pound pulled and discarded, another is cooked and eaten like spinach somewhere in the world where they recognize what we have forgotten – that it is a rich source of vitamin A and C and the mineral calcium. In the vegetable garden, pigweed will benefit sweetcorn, melons, cucumbers and squash, and push zinnias, pansies and marigolds to new heights of colourful extravagance. Now that is exactly the sort of weed we should all find space for.

Some years ago I was researching the sources of scent in the garden and came upon a charming book called *Delightes for Ladies to adorne their Persons, Tables, Closets and Distillatories.* Written by Sir Hugh Plat in 1609, it is a complete guide to what an Elizabethan lady thought necessary to improve the quality of her life, from 'Sugar scented of clove and cinnamon' to directions on how 'To make a paste of Violets, Roses, Marigolds, Cowslips or licorice'. This was my first introduction to cooking with flowers; who could resist?

The first flower to try is pot marigold (*Calendula officinalis*), known as the poor cook's saffron as the warm golden petals will colour food just as efficiently. Consequently, this humble cottage annual featured in every garden, and in medieval kitchens, in sweet and savoury recipes – hence the common name. One of the prettiest of these early 'receipts' is for eggs coddled in buttered ramekins beneath a scattering of fresh marigold petals. As the eggs set, the colour from the petals melts into the white like rays emanating from the sunny yolk. Dried marigold petals impart a mild turmeric flavour to stews and broths, and will enrich the creamy colour of vanilla ice cream if they are steeped in the sugar syrup base.

ABOVE *Lettuces come a close second to brassicas for colourful foliage, as demonstrated here by the frilled red-tinted leaves of 'Lolla Rossa'; other good reds include 'Red Oakleaf', 'Red Salad Bowl', 'Little Leprechaun' and 'New Red Fire', which makes slow-to-bolt, tight-leaved heads of frilled leaves. By planting hot-coloured zinnias and light green and blue green-leaved vegetables nearby, the redness of the lettuce is accentuated; the same effect can be achieved in the salad bowl, too!*

Cooking with flowers means more than simply tossing a few borage flowers and rose petals into a glass of Pimms, or scattering violets among the tossed lettuce leaves (go easy with violets, they have an emetic ability). Squash-flower fritters, daylily-bud tempura, nasturtium-bloom stir fry should all be experimented with; use your favourite batter recipe (as long as it is light and airy) and gather flowers that are on the point of opening. Do the harvesting when the sun has had a chance to dry the dew – wet blossoms make soggy fritters – inspect for insects, dip in batter, fry quickly and serve immediately. Purple chive flowers and white garlic chive flowers also make good fritters – although they're not annuals.

Squash and courgette flowers also make excellent containers for stuffing with a sweet and sour mix of pine kernels and chopped dates flavoured with a touch of cinnamon. Again use just-opened blooms and either sauté in sweet butter or dip in tempura batter to deep fry. One of the healthiest recipes using squash flowers comes from Alice Waters' *Chez Panisse Vegetables*, named for Waters' restaurant in Berkeley, California, where she makes the best possible use of a wide range of fruit and vegetables in season. It is for a risotto flavoured with summer squash and squash flowers. The squash (baby ones for preference) are diced and the flowers sliced into thin shreds across the bloom, to be added just as the rice begins to soften in the butter. Flavourings are added – sage, marjoram and savoury (annual summer savoury) would be my choice – then chicken stock and wine slowly stirred in until the rice is al dente. Polish with freshly grated Parmesan. Yum.

RIGHT *Beneath a morning glory-covered pergola, the gardener can relax in a flower-filled potager. Most usually, a potager plan follows the linear division of a plot into four equal squares bisected by main paths that cross at right angles to each other. Raised bed potagers, however, make much greater use of paths, since each bed is separate from its neighbours. Convention has it that the paths are edged in box or some other evergreen shrub, but in the modern potager we can take another leaf from history's text and edge paths with annual flowers like little lawn daisies, alpine strawberries, pot marigolds and so on. The trouble with this pretty idea is the difficulty of keeping such free-seeding plants to the borders. It is much better to use a vegetable edging, here a double row of red cabbages; the blue bloom of the foliage is a good foil for the morning glories.*

Borage flowers, both blue and white, will impart a distinct cucumber flavour to drinks, and the name 'Sops in Wine' given to an old-fashioned cottage garden pink refers to the use of this perennial to give wine a scent of cloves. The biennial sweet william, particularly the older varieties with the strongest scent, could serve the same purpose. Strip a flowerhead of its many small blooms, combine with a few borage flowers and add to a white wine cooler for a drink that is the essence of summertime.

In my part of the world, not far from the east coast of England, lemon grass will grow, but only as an annual. How I envy my Bahraini friends who grow it in huge evergreen clumps by the kitchen door, where the leaves are always handy for brewing the most refreshing tisane. Dried flowers of the half-hardy annual hibiscus are also used for the same purpose. Cardamom-flavoured sweetmeats often accompany these refreshments, and when enjoyed beneath the tamarind trees in a traditional Bahraini garden, with the waters of the Persian Gulf glistening in the background, it's close to tasting ambrosia in Paradise.

MAKING THE MOST OF COLOUR

By midsummer the soft pastels are turning to richer colours that bring depth and definition to all parts of the garden. Contrasts are enhanced and some beautiful visual effects can be obtained by playing the darker tones against lighter ones; when working with colour in the garden, it is the counterplay of colours and textures that make the picture interesting to look at.

One of the frequent criticisms of annual and biennial flowers is that they are gaudy. But this is because we have become used to seeing them in highly concentrated plantings of intense colour, where the difference of intensity between the hues has not been graduated. Put pure red next to bright yellow and the juxtaposition is harsh, but add a subdued burnt orange and the colours, while remaining bright and lively, interact more favourably; it's the difference between a shouting match and a lively conversation.

LEFT *A corner of the kitchen garden should always be devoted to flowers for cutting, for it is an important part of the gardening zeitgeist that part of every harvest should be profit as well as pleasure. Simple flower bunches or colourful mixed bouquets, heads of lettuce, bundles of carrots and surplus seedlings of annuals and biennials in strips or individual pots offered up in even the least pretentious manner will, nevertheless, prove an irresistible bargain to passersby, and the few pennies earned help to fund the next year's bounty. Such cottage-garden economy is based on finding the best plant for the purpose, such as the sweet william 'New Era', which flowers in its first year.*

RIGHT *Dwarf Nicotiana 'Havana Appleblossom' is bicoloured pink and white, blending perfectly here with soft pastel-coloured bracts of Salvia horminum 'Claryssa' and the heavily textured, veiny foliage of savoy cabbage.*

LEFT *The naturalized perennial garden demands a certain amount of weed freedom in its early establishment phases. Once the perennials have reached their mature size, their annual leaf growth will smother any weeds developing from winter-borne seeds, however, in the early stages there will be quite a bit of bare earth between plant groups, so the aim is to keep the soil covered with something that is non-competitive and attractive at the same time. Hardy annuals fit this bill admirably.*

When making the annual selection, always consider the soil, its ambient moisture levels and the amount of light the area receives, and choose the annuals accordingly.

Generally speaking, it will take three years to establish the perennials as a cohesive planting, so spacing need not be too dense. Using annuals to fill the gaps and suppress weeds does mean that you must thin the seedlings to allow them adequate space to develop strongly, especially if they are expected to compete with weeds.

Colours can be roughly grouped into three categories: colours that are adjacent to each other in the colour wheel and harmonize (red, orange, yellow); those that are opposite each other as complements (blue and orange, red and green, blue and yellow); and colours that are equidistant on the colour wheel, sometimes known as triads (red, yellow, and blue; green, orange and blue-violet; red-orange, violet and blue-green).

Pluck a flower and study it closely; the tints that it is made of will describe its colour companions. Flowers are rarely one solid colour; their veins or throats may be a darker hue or an entirely different colour; stems can be coloured also or the bracts may contain some shading in a harmonizing shade. Use these colours as a guide to which plants will work together.

LEFT As the summer matures, so do the leaf and flower colours; pastel tints subside beneath a tide of deeper tones as in this border where the main foliage interest comes from the broad oval leaves of Plantago major *'Rubrifolia', commonly referred to as bloody dock on account of the purple cast of the normally dull green foliage. Purple-leaved orache (*Atriplex hortensis var. rubra*) is another good dark leaf and both plants can become something of a weed as they will assiduously self-seed in almost any spot in the garden. These dark reddish colours provide good foundations for blue flowers like delphinium, as well as stronger reds and oranges as provided here by* Linaria *'Crown Jewels'. Hard cutting back after the first flush will keep linaria blooming late into the season.*

RIGHT Petunia *'Plum Purple', cherry pie (*Heliotropium peruvianum*), the tender perennial* Verbena rigida *and pink-flowered impatiens, or busy lizzie, make a rich-hued monochrome scheme for container-grown summer flowers.*

Generally, perennial foliage will be blue, blue-green, grey-green and so on, but there are many variegated-foliage plants and there are shades of copper-brown and russet-red, especially among grasses. Heucheras have purple foliage and near black can be had from *Ophiopogon nigrescens*. Unusual background colours like these can stimulate some truly inspired plant combinations, weaving together perennials and annuals.

Colour doesn't have to be used lavishly, either: a sprinkling of ruby-red or orange amid a predominantly blue and purple planting will enhance those colours and give the whole picture a lift, while a harmonizing scheme seems by comparison tranquil and visually undemanding.

How many times do you look at the world through rose-coloured glasses? Feel green with envy? Red with rage? Somewhere in the mists of time, our ancestors began associating colours with emotions as well as with social class, for example royal purple, and with rites of passage – black for mourning, white for weddings. Even animals, it seems, are

OPPOSITE *In a cloud of* Gypsophila elegans, *the soft lemon-yellow flowers of the evening primrose* Oenothera *'Lemon Gem' float gently with the ruddy pink tinge of their foliage accented by dots of pure red from corn poppies. This is a particularly fine form of a perennial evening primrose, but one which in my mild, temperate garden grows a self-seeding annual, never appearing in the same place twice, but always turning up in exactly the right spot!*

TOP LEFT *Complementary blue and yellow are featured in this group of annuals, with the bright blueness of the larkspur (*Consolida ambigua*) highlighted by the orange and yellow of chrysanthemum 'Primrose Gem' and simple* Anthemis tinctoria.

CENTRE LEFT *Soft green-flowered annual* Nicotiana *'Lime Green' and purple* Verbena rigida, *a tender perennial, form another complementary colour scheme. The dots of bright orangey-red from perennial* Lobelia cardinalis *are yet another complementary accent.*

BOTTOM LEFT *White gardens are a much-loved feature, and annuals and biennials are some of the finest small-flowered subjects to be used as fillers among the larger perennials; these little dots of colour are what hold the planting together. Here,* Incarvillea sinensis *'Cheron', a creamy-white hardy annual, blends with the snapdragon 'White Wonder', white-flowered gypsophila, white zinnias and the little daisy-flowered erigeron, commonly called Daisy gone crazy on account of its free-seeding habit.*

influenced by the colours in the world around them; chickens, apparently, have a preference for red over blue.

Colours have also acquired a mystical symbolism which can provide an extra layer of thought when contemplating the scheme for a garden. White-themed gardens are popular, white being the colour of innocence and purity, of joy and triumph. White is in fact the absence of colour, and can also signify death – ghostly ladies gliding through midnight glades usually being clad in white.

Black in gardens is a novelty colour and making an all-black garden using the ophiopogon cited above, along with black-flowered tulips, the little 'Bowles' Black' viola, frilly-petalled, black-flowered opium poppy, and any other plants with black leaves or flowers your research turns up could become a lifelong project, and a rather mournful part of the landscape! Black is the presence of every colour, but in garden plants it is usually an exceptionally deep, saturated reddish-purple. It signifies the powers of darkness and death, but can also be extremely restful – the darkness of a still night.

Purple is a regal colour while blue is the colour of wisdom, truth and divinity, and in love it is the colour of loyalty and devotion. Green carries many of the same

associations, except that in love it is traditionally the shade of jealousy and envy.

Yellow is the colour of joy and rebirth (no doubt because of the yellow sun reappearing each dawn, giving light and life to the earth) and of wealth and material well-being – gold is the child of the sun and silver that of the

LEFT Nemesia strumosa *'Blue Gem' and* Brachyscome iberidifolia *'Purple Splendour'*.

RIGHT Tagetes, *here 'Paprika', are annuals that are easy to grow, profuse in flower and have scintillating tints that make them so valuable in the midsummer garden, either reinforcing the schemes of perennial plantings or, informally sown, making a carpet of many colours.*

LEFT *Besides its action as a life-giving force, light is important in other ways, illuminating the garden and giving definition and depth to the plan and the plants.*

When we begin to design our gardens, the first thing we are told to do is watch the light, to know where it falls on the landscape and when; to mark where the deep shadows are as well as the sunniest parts of the garden. One of the best contributions light makes to the garden is when it cuts low across the landscape, either in the early morning or late afternoon. If there is a spot you can recognize as receiving the rays of the rising or setting sun, this is where to plant something eye-catching, particularly if it is a place that can easily be seen from the house or from the sitting-out areas. In my garden, I have put a flowering almond to make the most of the rising sun in early spring, and a liquidambar to catch the setting sun in its fiery autumn foliage. But even a simple frond of fennel when cross-lit by late-afternoon summer sun can be transformed into a thing of exceptional grace as the light catches the translucent wings that edge each leaf where it joins the stem. The greater garden picture is made up of details such as this, so hold that thought when sowing and planting, and keep your eye on the light.

moon. Yellow, however, has its weaknesses: cowardice, treachery and deceit.

Red is the colour of passion and the colour of life (blood-red), of energy and warmth (fiery red); and of sinfulness (remember Hester Prynne with the scarlet letter 'A' emblazoned on her bodice).

It is thought that these archetypal associations are what condition our emotional responses to colour – so that, most obviously, some colours seem more cheerful than others. Yellow is cheerful, red is passionate, and orange has a trace of each quality in its emotional make-up; blue is quiet and contemplative but violet mournful; green refreshes the spirit with its blend of tranquillity and optimism. Furthermore, in the terminology of colour theory, intensity refers to the degree of colour purity, while value describes how dark or light a colour is – the lower the intensity the darker the value; the higher the intensity, the richer the colour. The intensity and value of colour will also influence our emotional responses. By midsummer, the intensity of flower colour is increasing as the value is lowered, just as the intensity of the sunlight is heightened but the hours of daylight are gradually decreasing. Watching the garden change through the seasons, not just the summer, it is possible to watch this at work; colours become more and more intense: pale pink turns to dusky red, butter-yellow turns to burnished gold, and our spring-time rush of optimism becomes the full-blown pleasure of summer, turning eventually to the satisfying fulfilment of autumn.

When planning a colour-themed garden, be it an entire border or a simple bed of modest dimensions, it is possible

to exploit the emotional and physical properties of colour. A planting scheme for midsummer might, therefore, make use of the most intense tints of the warmest harmonizing colours, for example hot pink snapdragons, vivid yellow eschscholzia and fiery orange zinnias all with the same values, but try incorporating a shot of violet schizanthus or blue *Salvia nemorosa* as a complement, and the picture loses some of its heat with the introduction of their soothing cool blue tints.

Some of the best annuals for the midsummer garden have flowers in varying shades of red, and foremost among these must be the nasturtiums (*Tropaeolum majus*); varieties

and commented, 'the whole flower hath a fine small sent, very pleasing, which being placed in the middle of some Carnations of Gilloflowers [clove pinks] . . . make a delicate Tussimussie as they call it, or Nosegay, both for sight and sent.' Linnaeus, however, gave it the genus name *Tropaeolum*, by which we know it today, as the configuration of leaf and helmet-shaped flower suggested a classical 'trophy' of shield, spear and helmet; his daughter commented that she could see glowing sparks fly from its petals! There are species which, though somewhat tender, can be grown as perennials in a greenhouse or conservatory; the flame flower (*T. speciosum*) lives up to its name with clear scarlet flowers, while *T. azureum* has fine star-shaped foliage and azure-blue flowers and does best in a cool, moist atmosphere. *T. polyphyllum* is a hardy annual, however, with pink-tinged buds opening to bright yellow flowers on a compact plant.

In the garden, nasturtiums require little attention and flower best on lean ground; they can withstand periods of drought but are frequently ravished by blackfly and aphids. Nasturtiums are happy self-seeders; as William Robinson remarked, 'the rapid growth of the annual [sorts] is proverbial, and their hardiness in a temperature above freezing point, as well as their indifference to soil, makes them useful where anything unsightly is to be hidden.'

LEFT *Trailing nasturtiums with flat round leaves winds their way through the upright stems and feathery foliage of* Achillea *'Terracotta'; the only harmony between these contrasting plants is the hot colours of their flowers.*

are available with flowers of pale faded yellow, creamy buff orange, scarlet, crimson and dark mahogany-red. There are variegated foliage sorts and double-flowered varieties, trailing or bunching in form. One of the best and most saturated colour-wise is the old favourite 'Empress of India', with dark foliage and crimson flowers. 'Strawberry Ice' has good blue-green foliage which shows off the vivid yellow flowers, each petal of which is clearly blotched with red.

Nasturtiums, also known as Indian cress, came to Europe from South America via Spain. The English herbalist John Parkinson described a plant in his book *Paradisus in Sole, Paradisus Terrestris*, published in 1629, as *Nasturtium indicum*,

Snapdragons and mimulus are old cottage-garden stalwarts, although the snapdragon (*Antirrhinum majus*) is of much earlier introduction, coming originally from the Mediterranean regions to our gardens so long ago that in many places it has naturalized. During the mid-1800s the snapdragon became a Florist's flower – the florists being not purveyors of cut-flower arrangements, but amateur plant breeders whose goal was to produce the most perfectly formed specimen of a selected, or Florist's, flower. Auriculas are the best known Florist's subject, but snapdragons had their day too, and Florists bred veritable bushes, 1.5m (5ft) wide and 2.2m (7ft) tall. Highly contrasted, bicolour flowers were the ideal, but mottled, splotched and striped sorts were also shown.

We can grow stupendous snapdragons too, but only ones reaching heights of 1m (3¼ft) or slightly less, like 'Ruffled Super Tetra' or 'Liberty Mixed', which produces tight uniform flowerheads in the best traditions of the old Florists, who prized uniformity. But more appealing for the mixed border among perennials and shrubs are medium stature plants; the flower spikes look well making strong vertical accents among ornamental grasses with rounded, flowing forms. 'Black Prince' is superb for its intensely dark crimson flowers, or use 'White Wonder' for the opposite effect, while 'Purple King' falls in the mid-range with a rich lilac-purple colouring.

Mimulus was the cottage gardener's favourite windowsill pot plant, until it mysteriously lost its lingering sweet scent and was thereafter relegated to the border as a filler plant. It came to Europe from North America in the 1820s, full of perfume and promise which by the end of the century had been realized, with larger-flowered, better-shaped plants being bred, but with each generation losing more of its prized fragrance. Musk flower or monkey flower are its old common names.

Mimulus comes in shades of scarlet, orange or yellow, with 'Whitecroft Scarlet' said to be the finest red. *Mimulus lewisii* is a fine species with rosy pink flowers and maroon speckling in the throat.

Snapdragons do best on dry stony ground; mimulus prefer moist soil and partial shade, although *M. lewisii*

LEFT *The palmate, reddish-brown leaves of the castor oil plant (*Ricinus communis*) are a good foil to the smaller spots of colour provided by flowers like these dusky pink snapdragon spikes.*

RIGHT *Mimulus 'Red Emperor' shows off well against the red-tinged foliage of the lettuce 'Lollo Rossa'; the one occasion when I don't mind bolting is when lettuce is used as an ornamental plant, since the spike of colourful textured foliage contributes to the planting scheme.*

RIGHT *The doctrine of mass plantings for bold effect can be expounded beyond the confines of the herbaceous perennial border, or the drift planting of the naturalistic perennial garden. Bold annuals lend themselves to this kind of planting, especially flowers like the zinnia, which is not the easiest of mixers due to its vivacious colouring and assertive form. But in a border or drift on its own or with similar hot colours such as tagetes and salvias as here, it will shine, while planted with its compatriots the dahlia and the morning glory as a Mexican trio, it would be an exuberant scheme to warm the heart of any chill northern garden.*

Zinnias were just one of the many colourful flowering plants that the Aztec people grew in their elaborate gardens. Theirs was a highly civilized culture and horticulture was well advanced by the time the first Conquistadors arrived and almost at once began their plunder of the New World, sending back countless plants along with the gold and riches of the South American kingdoms. Linnaeus identified zinnias as Calthe de Bresil, the Brazilian marigold, and it came into cultivation in Europe in 18th century.

will tolerate some dryness and so can be grown in positions of dry shade.

Cheiranthus cheiri and *Dianthus barbatus* are hardy biennials that have held on to their scent through all the generations during which they have been grown in gardens. And, charmingly, both once shared the same common name of sweet william, probably because the wallflower (*Cheiranthus*) has the same spicy scent as the sweet william (*Dianthus*). Both were also favourite flowers for tussiemussies, the dainty little nosegays carried in the days when personal and public hygiene left much to be desired.

As biennials, these flowers are sown in spring to be moved to flowering positions in early autumn; they will come into flower in late spring along with tulips and early summer bulbs, and if cut back after the main flowering will give another burst of bloom. If the sweet williams are planted so that their lower flowering stems are beneath the soil surface, and the plants are well-watered and the soil fertile, the buried stems will develop roots and can be separated from the parent plant to increase stocks for next season. This is a William Robinson tip and is not always 100 per cent successful – which, of course, he would say was the fault of the gardener!

Violas also can be encouraged to root from layered stems, but will do so most easily from soft cuttings taken in midsummer. Dead-heading and hard cutting back after the

LEFT *A sympathetic blend of rosy reds and rich purples from biennial wallflowers dotted among the early season perennials, including dicentra and* Heuchera *'Palace Purple' can be continued through summer.*

CENTRE *Using red-flowered sweet williams and purple pansies, the blue-red theme continues beneath the feathery foliage of blue-flowered* Aconitum napellus.

RIGHT *A rosy little pansy, 'Imperial Blackberry Rose', mixes with the tiny dot flowers of the salad leaf claytonia and the blue bells of* Polemonium caerulum; *a pot-grown plant of* Heuchera *'Palace Purple' tucked into the group adds foliage support. Small vignettes like this, in which the size contrasts but the colour blends, can be used to decorate terrace gardens and containers, or can be repeated through the garden as a unifying marker. By making the selection from among annuals, the feature can be geared to harmonize with main themes.*

first flush of flowers will also help to keep the plants blooming into summer.

Many annuals come from the warm temperate regions of the world, a fact we easily forget when lumping all annuals as plants suitable only for early colour. Many of the best come from California, and were introduced to our gardens by a Scotsman named David Douglas, who in 1824 was sent by the Royal Horticultural Society to the northwest regions of the American continent. He sent back some of the best annuals we now grow: eschscholzias, godetias, mimulus, nemophilia and clarkias (which previously had been known only as herbarium specimens collected by Lewis and Clark on their Northwest Passage Expedition).

Clarkias flower for a long period, and are among the easiest of hardy annuals to grow. Their willowy, upright habit, and the elegant branching of the flowering stems makes them good cut flowers and great border minglers, looking exceptionally fine among broad-leaf perennials; the flowers are delicately double and look like so many tiny roses – which gives a lead to a suitable choice of companion, as clarkias will grow to 60cm (2ft) and would do well among low-growing or groundcovering bushes. Alternatively, the species *C. rubicunda* has a semi-prostrate habit and vivacious fuchsia-pink flowers freely produced over a long period.

Good blue-flowered plants are still highly prized, and when nemophila first appeared on the scene *N. menziesii* immediately became a must-have and was given the rather cloying common name of baby blue eyes. But it makes a wonderful front-of-border-filler plant, stretching its arms full of clear blue flowers among neighbouring plants and doing best in loose, free-draining soil.

N. maculata produces a couple of the best, or at least most unusually marked and coloured, annual flowers. There is '5 Spot', white with dark blue spots marking the

LEFT *The flowers of* Clarkia elegans *'Apple Blossom' look like little crumpled shreds of tissue paper; this is an excellent flower for cutting and its subtle pink colouring blends easily in the garden.*

RIGHT *Nemophila 'Penny Black' is more stridently coloured with its bold white-bordered, nearly black petals. Try it with it with dark foliage like the purple-leaved basil* Ocimum basilicum *'Dark Opal', a partnership that brings out the unusual colour qualities of each plant.*

centre edge of each petal; 'Snowstorm', which is white freckled with deepest purple-black, and 'Penny Black', with intensely dark purple flowers each petal of which is edged with silvery white. It looks stunning among silver foliage plants and is, as you might suspect, indispensable in a 'midnight garden'.

ABOVE LEFT *Red orache* (Atriplex hortensis *var.* rubra)*, has been a popular salad herb since at least the 16th century and is a prolific self-seeder. As you might expect from the colour, the fresh young leaves taste of beetroot, but it is also as pretty an addition to the flower garden as it is to the salad bowl. A mature plant will reach a height of 1.5m (5ft), the stem laden with clusters of toasty brown seed.*

ABOVE RIGHT *Texture is the main attribute of heliotrope foliage; the murky green leaves are deeply veined and have a rough, light-absorbing surface which, combined with the sweetly scented flower panicles, gives the plant a soft tactile appeal.*

LEFT *The palmate, bronze-purple foliage of the castor oil plant* (Ricinus communis) *is an invaluable foil to vivid red* Salvia splendens *and burgundy-tinted* Perilla frutescens, *all of which are among the most richly coloured annuals.*

ABOVE *The sharply defined variegated form of common winter cress,* Barbarea vulgaris *'Variegata', makes bright groundcovering rosettes that persist nearly all year round. It is a biennial but can be grown as a perennial, although the foliage is best on young new plants.*

TOP RIGHT *Green and white is a cool and sophisticated colour scheme, and there are a number of easy-to-grow yet sophisticated annuals that can help you to achieve the look; against a silvery grey background of* Artemisia ludoviciana *the green flowers of* Nicotiana *'Lime Green' and the species* N. langsdorffii *mingle with a green-flowered zinnia – the dahlia-flowered 'Envy Double' has parrot-green petals – and white bracts from* Salvia horminum *'Claryssa White'.*

CENTRE RIGHT *In a seemingly accidental and therefore natural-looking planting, the annual* Bidens *'Golden Eye' blends the warm colour of its glossy yellow flowers with a starry white umbellifer (the herbs chervil and coriander are among some of the umbelliferous annuals that produce these delicate flowerheads), the little poppy-seed pots and the lavender-tinted brush of a wild thistle.*

BOTTOM RIGHT *Bold annuals such as the purple-tinted* Angelica gigas *require a bold setting, such as the one provided by the clearly defined shapes of purple coneflower (*Echinacea purpurea*) and* Achillea *'Terracotta'. In the background the 1.2m (4ft) spikes of motherwort (*Leonurus sibiricus*) make a strong vertical accent.*

OPPOSITE *The charm of some flowers lies in the open airiness of their structure, like the winsome wands of the tender perennial* Cosmos atrosanguinea. *In cool climates where there are prolonged periods of freezing weather, the tubers must be lifted at the end of each season and overwintered with frost protection, to be replanted in the early summer. The dark flowers of this plant are scented with chocolate, visually echoed by the chocolate-coloured blossoms of the annual* Centaurea *'Black Ball'.*

A number of annuals and biennials have strikingly coloured foliage, while their flowers are rather shy and lacklustre although neither of these characteristics are often associated with this rainbow tribe.

Variegation takes many forms, and leaves can be striped, edged, mottled, splashed, and freckled with yellow, cream, white, dark brown or purple. You must decide for yourself whether or not the variegation makes the plant look eye-catching or simply diseased, which can be the case with some patterns, particularly the mottled sort, but then variegation is often caused by an inherited virus.

The point has been made repeatedly throughout this chapter that foliage is equally as important as flower colour, and, as with flower colour, some of the best ways of using good leafy plants is to create contrasts of shape, texture, or pattern – solids against variegated. So keep an open mind and factor foliage into the garden equation.

As the height of the summer season crests, the planning for the coming year begins. Thoughts about colour will still be at the forefront of most minds, but then there is still plenty to do in this year's garden, and those tasks must not be ignored.

Holidays are frequently taken near the end of summer, and provisions should be made to care for annual plants while you are away from home; many annuals will continue well into autumn if given encouragement now. So, if the weather has been dry, give them as thorough a watering as possible and keep the plants free of debilitating seedheads by regular dead-heading. Those plants you have chosen to save seed from can be singled out for special treatment by simply marking them with a raffia tie, knotted loosely around a stem.

During midsummer, too, the annual and biennial plants you may have raised as reserve plants can be lifted and

LEFT *The half-hardy annual* Verbena × hybrida *is a versatile plant for containers, informal borders and formal bedding schemes, and offers a good choice of bright colours in addition to the familiar purple form, shown here with a deep crimson petunia.*

CENTRE *Eschscholzia, or California poppy, is a top value annual, easy to grow and a prolific self-seeder. The foliage is deeply cut, lacy and coloured a faded eau de Nil that works well among brown foliage plants like halorages and carex. The flower colours too are a perfect foil for other warm tints, and although the pumpkin-orange form is the most common, there is now a wide range of tints from cream to Schiaparelli pink.*

RIGHT *Like the marigolds, nasturtiums are a simple flower with petals the deep hot colour so prevalent in midsummer. And, like the marigold, they act as a bio-friendly insecticide, drawing blackfly and aphids away from interplanted crops and onto their stems, which can be plucked off to remove the insect pests.*

moved into gaps in the borders, beds or containers. Water them well before you move them (which is best done in the late afternoon so that they have a chance to recover overnight), and then water them well again the next morning. Being on the spot with the watering can will help the young plants transfer successfully, so don't do this just before you leave for holiday!

Young plants of biennials and short-lived perennials that have been raised in seed trays should be ready to transfer into nursery beds to bulk up before being transferred to flowering positions in the autumn. Again, watering is crucial and the nursery beds should be kept moist, but never sodden; too much water will encourage leaf growth at the expense of flowering.

SUMMER FADES

Silly gardener! summer goes,
And winter comes with pinching toes,
When in the garden bare and brown
You must lay your barrow down.

Robert Louis Stevenson
The Gardener

The blaze of midsummer colour declines into a glowing ember with richly tinted annual flower colour and the warm tints of ripening seed, as though the garden had turned into nature's baking oven, preparing the treats for the season to come.

If during the spring and early summer you have made successional sowings of hardy annuals, the garden will continue to give pleasure well into late summer and autumn, right up to the first frosts. If the weather is particularly hot and dry, keep the seedlings well-watered; plants raised in trays or pots can be put into their late-summer flowering

positions, but there too they should be kept well-watered until established. Frequent cutting and dead-heading will remove developing seedpods and help to prolong the display of late summer flowers like larkspur, nicotianas, and sunflowers, and can even promote a second flowering period.

In his book *The Amateur's Flower Garden*, published in 1897, Shirley Hibberd praised hardy annuals: 'There is no other class of plants that can give an equal display of colour and an equal range of characters and colours, gay and various, for the small amount of labour required to produce a brilliant border of hardy annuals.' One hundred years later, anyone who has experience of growing annuals would agree with his assessment. Furthermore, the methods of cultivation have not changed: seedbeds raked to a fine tilth, seed sown evenly in shallow drills or individually if large enough, then covered over with a light blanket of sifted compost, watered, weeded and thinned – that is the recipe for success. Hibberd also stressed the need for early sowing,

LEFT *Many annuals attract butterflies and moths, particularly those of the Compositae family like this orange helichrysum.*

RIGHT *Nasturtium 'Peach Melba' fills a container formed by a clipped box parterre.*

PREVIOUS PAGE *By summer's end, there is a feeling of mellow abundance overtaking the garden, and with it comes a mellowing of colour; fiery reds fade to warm embers, sunny yellow is replaced with mellow gold. It is a time for reflection and repose, when there are few urgent garden tasks other than dead-heading and watering as necessary.*

the advantage being that plants then had the time to develop a sound root system and leafy superstructure that would support continuous and abundant flowering. Therefore, the advantage to late summer sowing is obvious: many seeds will lie dormant through the worst of winter and then germinate as the soil warms. The danger is that a sudden cold snap may nip developing plants, but if seed is sown where the young plants can be protected with traditional tunnel or barn cloches or 'fleece' covers, the gardener has the upper hand.

Most annuals prefer a rich, deeply dug soil. A dusting of lime before sowing can be beneficial, as can the addition of well-rotted compost or manure to sandy soil or leafmould

LEFT *Verbascum comes into its own at the end of summer, when the blank felted rosette that has hugged the ground for so many months finally sends out its towering flower spike and the single yellow flowers engulf the stem like a swarm of tiny butterflies. In this wonderfully effusive natural planting scheme, the verbascum and other tall-growing annuals and perennials create a sense of enclosure around a terrace next to the house. Intimate spaces like this one created by flowering walls are among the most soothing to the spirit. Sitting among the stems and blossoms you become absorbed into the life of the plants as the bees and insects busy themselves among the flowers, and the breeze releases the flower scent and the latent motion of the supple-stemmed plants. This is one of the most appealing qualities of the informal and naturalistic planting scheme – and most easily had by letting the flowers find their own place in the garden. So resist the temptation to plant by rigid rules of height; take the annuals out of their rows and let them loose to mingle freely with each other, and with you.*

to heavy soil. In tidy cottage gardens where annual flowers and vegetables rub shoulders in a formal layout, raised beds satisfy all the conditions for healthy growth. The beds will also be easy to cover against late frosts, and the free-draining conditions help the soil to warm more rapidly in spring.

Hardy annuals will survive winter cold, and for this reason many gardeners choose to sow them in the late summer or early autumn. But even as we busy ourselves with the garden here and now, we should keep an eye on the future,

taking cuttings of some tender annuals like heliotrope, ageratum, verbenas, double nasturtiums, abutilons and salvias. Soft cuttings taken from these plants, using young healthy shoots about 3–5cm (1¼–2in) long, will root readily. Remove the lower leaves and trim the stem cleanly across just below a leaf joint. Dip the cut end in hormone rooting powder (a fine dusting rather than a plastering of powder is all that is needed). Put the cuttings into pots of moist cutting compost (I generally add some extra horticultural vermiculite to make enhance the porosity of the compost), and put in a sheltered spot. Cover the pots with a plastic bag to make a mini-greenhouse. I also find that putting pots of cuttings in the shade of greenhouse-grown tomato plants works well; the shady, moist microclimate beneath the sheltering fronds is exactly what the baby plants need, and windowsills and staging are left free for other things.

Many annuals are at their prime late in the summer; these are usually natives of South Africa, South America and Mexico, as well as Southern California and the prairie states of the American Midwest. Most of these plants are also excellent as cut flowers, and while some must be direct-sown in the spring and will flower in late summer, others sown in late summer or early autumn will begin flowering in the early summer, and be encouraged to continue flowering by the constant cutting.

THE CUT-FLOWER BORDER

In the days when gardens were tended by teams of gardeners, under-gardeners, pot-boys and weeders, it was common practice to set aside an area of the vegetable

LEFT *There is a standard repertoire of foliage plants recommended for use beneath roses, but when the rose is a striking colour, I like to see it emphasized by equally outspoken companions; in this case fiesta-coloured zinnias, tithonias and perennial rudbeckia.*

RIGHT *In a much-admired kitchen garden, the decorative virtue of sweetcorn is underlined by its petticoat of tithonia – a New World partnership, as both these plants originate from South America.*

garden to grow flowers for cutting; greenhouses too provided cut flowers as well as flowering pot plants to decorate
the halls and reception rooms of country houses and town
mansions. Today you are probably fulfilling all the gardening roles yourself, and your flowers, herbs and vegetables
grow in companionable patches throughout the garden.
But where there is space, even if it is only a narrow ribbon
of soil along a path to the front door, you could grow an
annual cutting garden.

Use hardy annuals that you can sow now, and cover the
seed with horticultural fabric mulch to keep the seed
undisturbed by birds and beasts; it will also give the
seedlings a head start by keeping soil warm and moist.

Make a list of the annuals you intend to grow, grouping
them by colour and then height within each colour range;
it's rather like planning a perennial border, because the
plants are best arranged with tall subjects at the back, the

medium-height plants in the middle and short subjects
along the front. If the cutting border is long, it might be an
idea to put sweet-pea or climbing nasturtium wigwams at
intervals along its length.

Mark out the ground using silver sand to outline the
sowing areas. Firm the seed in well, water, and cover with
the mulch; this can be removed in early spring, by which
time many of the seedling should be growing strongly, and
others will begin to catch up. You may need to thin more
than once, unless you have a particularly light touch with
seed – aim for 5-8cm (2–3¼in) between each plant.

Some hardy and half-hardy annuals that are good for cutting are asters, cosmos, godetia, clarkia, Brompton stocks,
sweet william, sunflowers, pot marigolds and *Rudbeckia hirta*
'Green Eyes' and 'Kelvedon Star', mignonette (*Reseda odorata*), *Gaillardia pulchella*, *Crepis aurea*, *C. rubra* and 'Snowplume',
and *Coreopsis grandiflora* 'Early Sunrise' and 'Mayfield Giant'.

LEFT AND CENTRE *At a nursery garden in Holland, the annuals are grown in row upon colour-filled row as a 'pick your-own' crop; ready-gathered bouquets are also sold. This is a highly adaptable sort of enterprise, and one to which most gardeners could turn their hand. But even without an entrepreneurial edge, a few rows of annuals for cutting would repay the effort with their guileless charm, and few flowers have the innocence of the sunflower especially when presented in an unsullied bunch. Sunflowers in a mixed bunch also retain their beauty, and here shine amongst the blue-flowered borage, long-flowering Cynoglossum amabile 'Firmament', and zinnias.*

RIGHT *In another mixed bouquet, pure white snapdragons, cosmos and zinnias blend with umbelliferous dill seedheads, poppy seedheads and spent flower spikes of motherwort, supplemented by the bristly blue spheres of the perennial Echinops ritro. While growing rows of annuals dedicated to providing cut flowers may be the counsel of perfection and tasteful colour blends may be recommended as the* sine qua non *of bouquet assembling, the simplicity of annuals, their pure colour and unfussy forms make even the least considered posy more appealing than a florist's expensive masterpiece.*

Some annuals like *Plantago major* 'Rubrifolia', *Perilla frutescens* and *Bupleurum griffithii* 'Green Gold' are good foliage plants and should be included for cutting. Browsing through *Pot Pourri from a Surrey Garden*, written by Mrs C. W. Earle c.1875, I came upon this recommendation: 'The common Hemp (*Cannabis sativa*) is a lovely foliage-plant when well grown and not crowded up.' She is absolutely correct, but of course we are now forbidden to grow this attractive and useful plant (flax linen is a highly durable fabric made from hemp); opium poppies, too, are on the proscribed lists of some gardening nations, which is too bad given the beauty of the flower, foliage and seedpod.

SEED COLLECTING AND SEEDHEADS

At the end of summer, flowerheads begin to turn to seed. In the case of most hardy annuals, once it is shed it begins to germinate almost immediately. Given enough moisture

RIGHT, TOP TO BOTTOM *Annuals are container-garden stalwarts. Here a cherry-red petunia grows with dark green ivy; dwarf nicotiana and nasturtium in shades of red are teamed with blue felicia; and a standard-size nicotiana in shades of white and green has grey-leaved ballota for foliage background.*

OPPOSITE *When the container is as dramatic as this urn and pedestal, the planting must match it in character, an effect admirably achieved with a cockade of cleome supported by glaucous blue cabbage plants and the deep red leaves of* Perilla frutescens.

LEFT, TOP TO BOTTOM *Cottage-garden economy demanded that gardeners be frugal and save their own seed from year to year. But this will not work with hybrids, so confine your seed-saving to species and old-fashioned flowers that you know will come true. Use paper bags for small quantities of seed or, for large amounts, use a sealable, clean glass jar. The seed must be kept moisture-free.*

OPPOSITE *Sunflowers are a favourite cottage-garden annual, and there are many named cultivars such as 'Valentine' and hybrids such as 'Sunbeam' available. Sunflowers should be sown in their flowering positions, two or three seeds in each spot, to be thinned to one plant. Exploit their strong vertical habit and stout stems to create living fences and supports for climbing annuals like runner beans or nasturtiums.*

and light, the seedlings will develop into strong and healthy plants before winter chills bring on dormancy. With the return of spring, warm showers and lengthening days, the plants resume growing, and come into flower in late spring and early summer.

Left to their own devices, hardy annuals will seed themselves quite happily, appearing wherever the breeze carries them. In my kitchen garden, an initial sowing of Shirley poppies, made several years ago near the entrance gate, has 'walked' to the other side of the garden, without any assistance from me.

Save seed from only the healthiest, finest-looking plants, tagging the ones you've selected so that they can be distinguished from their fellows later on. Collect the seedpods on a still day after the sun has dried away any lingering morning dew, and have labels ready so that each sort can be

named as you work – no matter how good you think your memory is, it will never be good enough to identify correctly a dozen different sorts of seed once they're spread on the workbench. If the pods are gathered before they are completely ripe, cut them with a length of stem, wrap them in a labelled paper bag and suspend the bunch upside down in a warm room to ripen. The pods will burst and the seed will be collected in the bag. Always use paper bags, envelopes or glass jars for storage, never plastic bags as seed must be able to 'breathe' to prevent it from going mouldy.

Hardy annual plants raised from autumn-sown seed are more robust, so provided space is available, it is worth making a seedbed in a quiet, sheltered corner of the garden where you can raise self-sown seedlings collected from the garden or else make fresh sowings of a few of the old-fashioned cottage-garden favourites such as mignonette, limnanthes, candytuft and Virginia stocks, which can be planted out as gap-fillers among perennials in the early summer. Some tender annuals, for example morning glories, will produce bigger and earlier-flowering plants if

LEFT *A garden with naturalized annuals, both flowers and grasses, will never be without interest. The blend of seedheads, late flower colour, shapely foliage and graceful forms is a truly soothing sight, particularly when the grass foliage responds to the breeze while the insects and birds such a planting attracts busily forage for pollen and seeds. Here, the vermilion-red fingers of love-lies-bleeding (*Amaranthus caudatus*), reach into the emerald grass leaves. Another colour accent comes from the purple corymbs of* Verbena bonariensis, *which for my money is one of the best plants in the late summer garden, working especially well in the grassy matrix.*

RIGHT *The curving flowerhead of* Setaria macrostachya *illustrates the elegance of the annual grasses; eye-catching sculptural effects can be obtained by combining it with similarly shaped flowers – like the amaranthus opposite – or other clearly defined forms such as ball-shaped flowers like those of* Echinops ritro.

ABOVE LEFT *The seedheads of common green-leaved orache are just as attractive as those of its red-coloured relative; here it is growing among the rounded seed umbels of dill, and with white zinnias and golden marigolds.*

ABOVE RIGHT *Pendant seeds are especially attractive, and none are as beguiling as the little beetle-like papery seeds of quaking grass (Briza maxima), an annual grass that self-sows freely in most soils. In early spring its tufts of broad blades are easily distinguished from unwanted weed grasses.*

they are sown in trays or pots in late summer and over-wintered under glass.

Some of the annuals and biennials we grow have been garden favourites for centuries, and these are generally species; flowers like *Calendula officinalis* (pot marigold), or *Atriplex hortensis* var. *rubra* (red orach). These are the seeds that are worth saving because they will reliably come true each year. It is not worth saving seed from named garden cultivars, or from F_1 or F_2 hybrid plants, as these are the product of chance crossings in the garden or else professional breeding programmes aimed at producing a brighter flower, a more vigorous plant or finer flavour. Such seed

will produce plants but they will be different from their parent. So, to be sure of having your favourite flower each year it is important to buy fresh seed, or, as in the case of an especially selected form, like the nasturtium 'Red Wonder', you can raise new plants from soft cuttings.

In the previous sections I have made the point (repeatedly, I admit, but it is important) that seedheads make a considerable contribution to the garden, and that late in the season they can be the main focus. This is especially true of annual grasses. Their flowers and foliage during the early part of the summer can be used to provide a green matrix through which other more decorative and obvious annual

ABOVE LEFT *Like its flowers, the rounded seedheads of safflower* (Carthamus tinctorius) *are good for drying, and planted to mature among spikelets of small seeded plants can bridge the gap between summer and autumn. If left in place and weather permitting, they can even take the garden through to winter.*

ABOVE RIGHT *Never underestimate the charm of the commonest annual, such as the red-leaved orache; the red colouring lingers as the seeds turn to golden toasty brown and it makes a pretty showing with the cold silvery grey of* Artemisia *'Powis Castle'.*

flowers can grow, but late summer is when they will come into their own with tassels, tufts, plumes and brushes of fine seed, the dainty flowery husks faded to shades of tawny gold, dusty beige and palest celadon-green. But the colour is never the strong point; rather it is the continuing interest to be gained from the form and texture of the plants.

Annual grass seed can be sown in situ: don't broadcast the seed as you would a new lawn, but sow it in shallow drills drawn in a sinuous line through the planting area. Seed for hardy annual flowers can be mixed with the grass seed or sown independently. Drill sowing also makes it easier to sort the weed seedlings from the desirable grass seedlings.

Alternatively, seed can be sown in plugs, small pots or trays for pricking out into growing positions; after the seed has germinated the seedlings should be thinned to 3–6 per pot, depending upon the mature size of the grass – the larger the grass the fewer seedlings per pot. Grown like this, grass plants can be dotted into the border among perennials and other annuals.

Most annual grasses, and the tender perennial grasses, which are easiest if they are treated like annuals, enjoy a sunny, open position in the garden; in warm-region gardens some of these annual grasses can become invasive if left to self-sow.

Top of my list of must-haves is quaking grass (*Briza maxima*). The tufts of pale green foliage appear very early in the spring, so it is a good foliage foil among early-flowering bulbs like dwarf daffodils and irises; by midsummer the wire-thin flowering stems are hung with the dangling panicles of glossy oval spikelets; these curious little seedheads look like some sort of beetle. In late summer, I scatter the seed among perennials near the front of the border and then thin and transplant seedlings in early spring.

Hordeum jubatum, commonly called squirrel tail barley or fox tail barley, has long silky flower spikes on erect stems; the unripe spikes have a pretty pink cast, but they ripen to rich golden-brown. Hare's tail (*Lagurus ovatus*) is aptly named, as the oval flowerhead is white and fluffy. Hair grass (*Aira elegantissima*) has the finest spreading panicles of tiny seed spikes on filament stems and consequently contributes a cloudy, misty mass to the border. It grows from a tuft of foliage to about 30cm (12in) tall.

Crimson fountain grass (*Pennisetum setaceum*) is a tender perennial that will grow to nearly 90cm (3ft) in a warm summer. The bottlebrush flowerhead is tinged with purple

LEFT *The collection of composite annual flowers growing through the mist of* Hordeum jubatum *includes* Rudbeckia hirta, *a perennial that is usually grown as an annual in cool climate gardens, and* Coreopsis tinctoria; *the darker centre markings of each plant are another unifying link in this bright planting scheme.*

RIGHT *Layers of contrasting and harmonizing colour are seen in this grouping of* Salvia patens *'Oxford Blue' purple* Verbena rigida, *orange tithonia and a hummock of dwarf marigold.*

at the core and doesn't mature until quite late in the summer. *Panicum miliaceum* 'Violaceum' is another tall-grower, to 90cm (3ft), with a showy bright green millet-type flower head that ripens to dark purple.

Zea mays is the familiar sweetcorn, and there are various ornamental sorts available, including the multi-coloured seedheads of Indian corn, where each kernel is a different shade of red, yellow, platinum and purple. There is also strawberry corn, which produces stubby little cobs of tiny garnet-red kernels. Of course, the beauty of these seedheads is only apparent when the ears are harvested and the husks pulled back, and then they can be used to make a feature on the harvest table, along with ornamental gourds and pumpkins.

DECORATIVE DRIED FLOWERS

For many people the main reason for cultivating annuals is to have the materials on hand to make floral decorations, either as a pretty pastime that also results in gifts for friends, or as a money-making cottage industry.

There are many annual and biennial flowers and grasses that are suitable for drying, and some of them even grow 'ready-dried' – or at least that it is how it seems. These are the 'everlastings', so called for their crisp, papery petals which are borne atop turgid green stems and leaves. The first time I encountered these curious flowers was as a small child, walking along the seafront at Dun Laoghaire, south of Dublin. I couldn't figure out who could be scattering

LEFT *The little bells of lime-green* Nicotiana langsdorffii *ring a bright note through the crisp brown teazel heads. This particular species of tobacco plant is worth seeking out; the upright branches are laden with pendant green flowers throughout late summer to the first frost, and it then liberally seeds itself around.*

CENTRE *The broad leaves and delicate tubular flowers of the woodland tobacco plant* Nicotiana sylvestris *are the anchors to a relaxed grouping of grasses, including* Pennisetum setaceum, *and annuals like tithonia, zinnia and the famous red orach.*

RIGHT *The standard tobacco plant for most gardeners is* Nicotiana alata, *which is widely available in mixed colours of white, rose, pink, purple and lavender. It is strongly perfumed and releases the scent at dusk, attracting moths to fertilize it and gardeners to admire it.*

artificial flowers along the grassy embankment, but thought it very generous of them to try to prettify the rather sombre harbour.

Strawflowers, species and cultivars of *Helichrysum*, a the most widely grown everlasting. Native to Australi *H. bracteatum*, from which the Montrosum Series pr really tall-growing plants, up to 1.2m (4ft). Flo generally rich russet-reds, burnt-orange, sulph and white, but 'Summer Solstice' has pale ti colours and 'Dargan Hill Monarch' has 5c flowers like papery sunflowers. *H. cassi* Pride' bears clusters of small white-petall central golden boss; the species is pink

TOP RIGHT *Vertical interest is emphatically made with a generous self-sowing biennial, Verbascum olympicum; its shorter relation with white flowers, V. chaixii 'Album', is a perennial. Elements of form and shape are just as important to an annual garden as they are to a perennial planting scheme, and it is just as well to be mindful of this when ordering seeds. A few vertically emphatic plants can make the difference between a 'ho-hum' show and a memorable planting mix.*

CENTRE RIGHT *The genus Oenothera, the evening primrose, includes some wonderfully coloured annuals, biennials and perennials that seed freely into well-drained sandy soils. Most have flowers that open only at night. Night gardens, or at least early evening gardens, are a genre suited to hard-working gardeners who find that the best time for horticultural activities is after the office has closed. Selecting evening-flowering plants and those that release their perfume at dusk make after-hours garden work a real pleasure.*

BOTTOM RIGHT *A vivacious late-summer planting makes use of the yellows and oranges from marigolds, tithonia, coreopsis, evening* ̶primrose and red orach. The key to annuals gardens is, to my mind, the ̶ ̶and dotting of plants, whereas in a traditional scheme the ̶ ̶nized into blocks or tight groups: like with like. Colours ̶ ̶ such plantings and each section is viewed in its ̶ ̶annuals are highly sociable, and by late summer ̶ ̶ls can have a cocktail-party air of gay abandon.*

̶ ̶ngled among annuals and perennials bring ̶ ̶With their sinuous stems and filamented ̶ ̶rens of the flower garden, snaring flowers ̶ ̶ng diverse annual and perennial flowers in ̶ ̶ the slightest breeze and spotlit in the late*

Pink daisy-flowered *Helipterum roseum* (syn. *Acroclinium roseum*, *Rhodanthe chlorocephala* ssp. *rosea*), also an Australian native, is half-hardy and needs to be started with bottom heat in the spring. *H. manglesii* (syn. *Rhodanthe manglesii*), however, can be sown outdoors in a sheltered spot in mild climates. *Ammobium alatum grandiflorum* is also Antipodean; each wiry stem carries several small daisy flowers with yellow button eyes and corollas of tiny white petals.

Statice (*Limonium sinuatum*) and pink pokers (*L. suworowii*, syn. *Psylliostachys suworowii*) are half-hardy annual natives of the Mediterranean. The first, with tapering sprays of small purple, blue, yellow, white or pink flowers, is most often encountered, although it is more difficult to grow successfully than its aptly named sister. *Xeranthemum annuum*, commonly dubbed harrisonia, has composite flowers in shades of pink, purple and white; although a half-hardy native of the sunny Med, it can be sown outdoors in spring.

Two really striking annuals for drying are safflower (*Carthamus tinctorius*) and bells of Ireland (*Moluccella laevis*). The former is a Mediterranean plant, with a ruff of bright green bracts surrounding a tight onion-shaped flowerbud that opens to a pompon of bright orange or yellow petals. It is half-hardy and in a warm location and good soil can grow to more than 1.2m (4ft). The latter gets its common name from its pure green colour (it actually is a native of central Asia), and it is hugely popular with flower arrangers for this characteristic. It is also half-hardy.

Larkspurs, cornflowers, eryngiums, amaranthus, love-in-a-mist, ageratum, asters, Canterbury bells, celosia, clarkia, drumstick scabious (*Scabiosa stellata*), meadow camomile, Brompton stocks, clary sage, honesty and

LEFT *Beneath a small tree, red and green are the colour theme of planting scheme composed of* Nicotiana *'Lime Green',* Centaurea *'Black Ball', the dark reddish-black foliage of perilla, and a dark red, old-fashioned snapdragon, 'Black Prince'. The dusky pink flower is a species nicotiana,* N. glutinosa.

CENTRE *Different tints of red and green in a planting of* Nicotiana langsdorffii *and* Alonsoa *'Firestone Jewels', a half-hardy annual.*

RIGHT *Glaucous blue-green nasturtium foliage is a good foil for shades of red, such as found in* Nicotiana *'Red Devil' and the bicoloured half-hardy* Nemesia *'Melo Red and White'.*

poppies can all be dried for either their flowers or seed-heads, or both. Add to this collection most of the grasses mentioned above, as well as a smattering of perennials, and you have quite a bit of vegetation from which to select the components of a bouquet, wreath, garland or simple posy.

By setting aside a part of the garden for dried-flower production, you can grow the plants in rows according to the type of flower or foliage, and use netting supports stretched horizontally over the bed; as the flowers grow, the netting can be raised up the supporting stakes to ensure that the stems of tall-growing annuals are grown as straight as possible.

Sow hardy annuals in rows in the late summer or early autumn, and half-hardy sorts in the spring either under glass with bottom heat, or else outdoors under cloches. Keep the rows weed-free by regular hoeing and mulch to help retain moisture. It is not a good idea to water the

TOP RIGHT Godetia rubicunda shamini, *amaranthus,* Clarkia elegans *'Apple Blossom' and a selection of annual grasses compose a gentle planting scheme of loose upright shapes against a formal hedge background. Apart from their blending abilities, grasses have a textural quality lacking in other plants. Here, it is the open airiness of the grasses that provides the leitmotif for a plant grouping.*

CENTRE RIGHT *The fringed buttons of ageratum and the filamented plumes of pennisetum share a feathery texture. Details are important; "don't ignore the small stuff" is a motto for any gardener to live by, as it is in the minutiae of nature that the greatest charm can often be found. A magnifying lens can be your best companion in the garden to observe flower structure – and colour – in macro-detail.*

BOTTOM RIGHT *The topiary evergreen sits like a sculpture on a pedestal of bright pink-flowered sedum; the sinuous arm of* Onopordon arabicum *reaching into the scene also has a clearly defined outline. Such elements help to bring definition to the gloriously naturalized planting all around.*

OPPOSITE *A floral feast of petunias, phacelia, asters and the curious spikes of* Ambrosia mexicana. *This grouping displays all the qualities of contrast to be had by playing off the varying elements of texture, form, colour and size found among the annuals tribe. To get your eye into this compositional frame, observe how plants come together in the wild and note the companionships that are formed. These partnerships can then be repeated in the garden using hybrid and garden-worthy relatives of the naturally occuring plant biomes.*

than when they are fully open, after which the colour begins to fade rapidly and will continue to do after gathering. Grasses, particularly, seem to be more fragile as they age – after all, the seeds are spread by shattering the head – and should be gathered when still green.

Gather the flowers on a warm day when there is a little breeze blowing and all the morning dew has evaporated; your aim is dried flowers, not fodder. Most will be cut with long stems and should be collected in small bunches held together with rubberbands which will contract as the stems shrink in drying. Remove all the lowest leaves from the stems, as these would only rot if gathered in the bunch.

Strawflowers are generally wired soon after gathering, as the stems when desiccated will not support the weight of the flowerhead. So, snip or pinch these off and collect in baskets (pinching will stain your fingertips). Several hours after gathering, pick over the flowers removing any leaves and snipping off stem remnants to leave just a short stub. Cut lengths of florist's wire (for small flowers use fine gauge,15cm/6in long; for large flowers use medium gauge, 30cm/12in long), and push through the centre of the stem stub and into the base of the flower, taking care not to push the wire all the way through the flowerhead. Gather the wired heads into small bunches and tie together.

plants, unless you have absolutely no choice; watering can be difficult to get right, and plants generally seem to colour better and be sturdier if they are grown 'mean and lean'.

Choose the time to pick each sort of flower according to its maturity; in many cases, the colour will be retained better in flowers that are gathered just before their peak

LEFT *Pink-flowered centaurea,* Clarkia *'Snowflake',* Salvia horminum *'Claryssa Rose' and corncockle in a monochromatic selection.*

RIGHT *More strident tints of the warm colours take off from a foreground of the curiously named 'Phlox of Sheep'; other flowers are snapdragons 'Liberty Mixed' and a shell-pink, single-flowered dahlia.*

The gathered flowers must be dried in a cool, airy place, out of direct sunlight and absolutely dry. That is the counsel of perfection. Hang the bunches upside-down, in well-spaced rows so that air can circulate freely around each bunch. When drying masses of flowers, it might become necessary to reduce the ambient humidity; this can be done by setting out trays of moisture-absorbing (and expensive) silica gel or by using a small domestic or greenhouse fan heater set to blow only cold air. Don't think to be clever and blow hot air into the room to speed the process; it will simply cause the flowers to open too much, to shatter or to become so brittle as to be crumbly to the touch.

Storage should be in a dark, well-ventilated room, suspended from wires stretched like washing lines across the ceiling, or else in small, loose groups in cardboard boxes, layered with tissue paper. As soon as light reaches the flowers, though, they will begin to fade.

The art of arranging these flowers, like that of arranging fresh flowers, is too complex to be tackled in these pages, but it may interest flower-arranging gardeners to hear what Lady Constance Lytton wrote on the subject as an appendix to *Pot Pourri from a Surrey Garden*, written by her cousin Mrs Earle:

'To the Japanese every flower has its meaning and associations, as well as every combination of flowers. The force of contrast is ever present in their designs . . . strength and weakness, sternness and tenderness, &c. Without learning the grammar of their complicated flower-language, might we not nevertheless increase our artistic pleasure in flower arrangements by trying to give them a suitableness and a meaning which have hitherto lacked? The old, long established English fashion of massing together in a vase may still hold its own for certain kinds of flowers; but, so strong is the fascination of the Japanese principle, that, once it is

LEFT *Cosmos are tried and true cottage-garden annuals, and the cultivar 'Sunny Lemon Twist' is one of the brightest, truest yellows in the garden. Here it is grown with* Tagetes *'Lemon Gem' and* Eschscholzia *'Milky White'. Planting partnerships like this one can be transferred to mixed floral arrangements, as so many annuals make ideal cut flowers, fresh or dried.*

CENTRE *Mass planting for colour effect using* Nicotiana *'Lime Green' and* Centaurea *'Black Ball'. Generous sowing of easy-to-grow annuals like nicotiana and cornflowers mean that you can gather cut flowers from the border. The alternative, of course, is to grow the annuals in rows as part of the vegetable garden or else in an area designated as the cutting garden.*

RIGHT *A pale pink form of* Verbena bonariensis, *grown with* Artemisia *'Powis Castle', one of the finest artemisias for foliage value. Its silvery grey colouring and lacy-cut leaf is especially good with pastels, but also provides good contrast with dark reds and purples both in the garden and in the vase.*

adopted, it will probably assert its authority even amongst a bunch of Primroses or Violets.'

THE SPIRITUAL GARDEN

Clearly, Lady Constance was advocating a simpler, more contemplative style of flower arranging, and it is interesting to note that more that one and half centuries later, we gardeners – and floral display artists – are looking for a more spiritual language in our designs. We search for the soul of the garden and try to establish its sense of place by evaluating the site and habitat and letting that dictate our plant choices to create a garden space that is in harmony with itself and its surroundings. So many of the gardens featured in this book have been made to this criterion, and although the plantings and layout have all the sophisticated complexity of a studiously 'designed' garden, a close assessment reveals that they are continuously designing and defining

RIGHT *Of the many annuals and biennials and half-hardy plants that came to the Old World from South America, few reached the popularity of the dahlia. But this native of Mexico was slow to take off; it was not introduced to Europe until 1789, and breeding of new varieties did not happen with any great urgency until, so it is said, the Empress Josephine took an interest. Throughout the years of the Napoleonic Wars she gardened assiduously, even importing plants from England via special courier. Among her collection were dahlias developed by French horticulturalists.*

Dahlias will grow as perennials outdoors in warm gardens and may also survive winter in a sheltered sunny spot in cool climate gardens. But in most northern gardens dahlias are frost tender, and so the tubers must be lifted in autumn to overwinter in a frost-free place. In the spring, when new shoots appear, the tubers can be divided and replanted, or the shoots can be removed and rooted to increase stocks.

There are single-flowered sorts, doubles, pompons, cactus-flowered (so-called for their spiky petal formation); dwarf and tall-growing with every size in-between in colours from white to midnight purple. With their substantial form and exuberant flowers, they work really well with finer-flowered annuals.

themselves, with the only external intervention being the garden-maker's initial plant selection, foundation planning and planting and ritual maintenance.

These gardens, and others like them, have a separate existence, one which is quite different from the more formal and traditional gardens, where the 'garden picture' is composed as if on the two-dimensional surface of a canvas or watercolour block, a pictorial style that treats the garden as an artefact, as though it is a museum exhibit and we are observers. Naturalistic gardens, where nature is the model and annuals and perennials are given their creative freedom, engage us more intimately. These gardens have a spirituality that we can become part of and through which we express our own aspirations and sentiments, working in a way that engages our passions, whether they are for colour harmony, or spiritual harmony. We can be 'in' the garden, as well as 'of' the garden.

Some time ago I came upon a very interesting little article by the garden historian Eleanour Sinclair Rohde on making a Shakespeare garden, using all the annual and

perennial flowers and herbs mentioned by the Bard in his plays and sonnets. In a square garden Eleanour proposed a formal plan of rectangular beds, each one planted with a different rose ('York and Lancaster', musk roses, cinnamon roses, cabbage roses), lavender, florentine iris, and so on, all underplanted with violets, pansies, columbines and marigolds of the common pot marigold sort (*Calendula officinalis*), also included in the quote Eleanour chose for its flowery beauty:

> Her eyes, like marigolds, had sheathed their light,
> And canopied in darkness, sweetly lay,
> Till they might open to adorn the day.

All was not sweetness and light in this Shakespeare garden, however, for there was a corner devoted to aconite, one of the deadliest herbs in the medieval pharmacopoeia, mandrake, ferns (to make witches invisible), and lethal hemlock.

Charmed by this idea, I continued to research and came upon an idea for making a Shakespeare garden using only

LEFT *The conical flower of silvery-blue* Eryngium giganteum *is repeated by the purple flower of* Agastache foeniculum, *making a visual statement about form rather than one purely about colour. This sort of effect can be organized by the gardener, but in my garden at least I find there are so many other things to be considered and remembered that planting so subtly often escapes me; it is often easier – and more successful – to rely on Mother Nature to be the garden designer.*

RIGHT *A simple pink-flowered cosmos catches the morning mist. Early morning in late summer is often the moment when gardeners get the first sniff of chill autumn weather.*

LEFT *With summer drawing to a close, the various annual elements of the garden take on a different guise. This is most notable among the grasses, with the brown ripeness of their seedheads and the topsy-turvy tumult of the border as stems bend to the wind and weight of seed bearing. Now is the time to begin the annual collection of seed, to clear patches of ground so that self-sowers can get a foothold, and to cut back and dead-head, seeking to prolong the flowering period.*

This is the time of year, too, when I find it useful to take a notebook into the garden to sketch ideas for next year's planting, to list the vegetable successes and note the all too many failures. But gardening is a ceaseless learning process – and that is its attraction. The more you learn the more you realize how much remains to be discovered, to be experimented with, and to be enjoyed.

Annuals, with simple directness, are among the best teachers in the garden; from them you can learn all the tricks of horticulture and design in the wonderfully enjoyable schoolroom of your own garden.

the 'weeds' he mentioned; nettles, buttercups and so on. The reference is now lost, but not the memory. Which is just as well, since so much of my garden-making, and that of other gardeners, is informed by memories: gardens we knew as children frequently inspire our efforts; or perhaps it was an historic garden which moved us so fundamentally that we wish to capture its spirit in our own design. Or perhaps it is just a single plant that, like Miss Wilmott's ghost (*Eryngium giganteum*), recalls a place, a time or an emotion keenly felt, and we sow the seed to rekindle the flame.

The language of flowers has persisted for centuries; in ancient China, Classical Greece, Medieval Europe, throughout the Persian Empire, and in Victorian England, the symbolism of flowers was recorded by scholars and poets and practised by romantics in every age. Each plant had its meaning, often reflected in the common name. Thus, amaranthus, with its limp, blood-red flowers, became known as 'love-lies-bleeding', but it was also a flower of immortality, the name meaning 'undying', because, like other late-summer flowers, this one can be dried and preserved to retain its summer richness in the midst of winter.

I grow the white-flowered form of the *Impatiens grandulifera* (syn. *I. roytei*), a giant relative of the busy lizzie which we know so well, as a container plant or groundcover plant for dry shade. In early spring, the seedlings appear, each seed leaf the size of a thumbnail. As summer progresses, the balsam begins its skyward climb, finishing up at about 1.8m (6ft) and bearing masses of pure white hooded flowers. It looks magnificent among the variegated dogwoods beneath a copse of Italian alder. It is also called 'touch-me-not' since the seedpods, when ripe, burst with an audible 'pop' at the slightest touch. The seed finds its way into most parts of the garden, so you do have to keep a watch on where it puts itself.

Thistles signify sternness; the quaking grass (*Briza*) means frivolity; evening primrose reveals inconstancy; sweet sultan tells of happiness; the sunflower admits to false riches; the little lawn daisy is all innocence and purity.

By summer's end the trees and flowers are fading, the dead and fallen leaves signifying, not surprisingly, melancholy and sadness. The daylight hours become shorter, and evening mists have a distinct chill, settling dew on ripening fruit and seedheads. The colours at this time of year are rich and ripe: apple-red, wheaten-gold and pumpkin-orange, and the low sun spotlights the warmest colours in annuals that originate in Mexico and Latin America.

LEFT *One packet of love-lies-bleeding (*Amaranthus*) and you will become hooked on these elegant, unusual and marvellously coloured annuals. Reading from the top row, the varieties shown are 'Intense Purple', 'Golden Giant', 'Love Lies Bleeding', and 'Green Thumb'.*

RIGHT *Amaranthus cruentus 'Golden Giant' growing with euphorbia and yellow-flowered* Oxalis chrysantha.

One of the best of these is *Tithonia rotundifola*, the Mexican sunflower. It is a truly splendid plant, tall-growing to 1.2m (4ft), with an open branching habit and soft, burnt-orange to terracotta-red flowers. It looks well grown with tall grasses or scattered throughout a block of sweet-corn, ripening in the potager. Nicotiana also comes from South America, as does the dahlia and the many species of tender salvias.

Blue seems always to be a rare colour among flowers, whatever the season, so a good tint is to be treasured – and such can be found with *Commelina dianthifolia*. From Mexico, it looks like a small tradescantia, but has wonderful deep gentian-blue flowers and a pleasing sprawling habit and will work its way among low-growing neighbours. It is a half-hardy annual but will seed itself around, so that once sown, always grown. I grow it with a coppery brown-leaved plant from New Zealand, *Haloragis erecta* 'Rubra', a

LEFT One of the most alluring late-summer plantings I have ever enjoyed was this fading display of tithonia, red-leaved orache and alliums. The coloured upright stems were hung with seeds and flowers, creating a screen of great depth and mystery in one quiet corner. There is much to be said for not being too tidy about the garden: leaving plants to fade in situ provides you with the chance to study their habits and to discover which ones have the most to offer for late summer colour and texture.

RIGHT Cosmos 'Sunny Orange Red' is one of three sisters, the others being 'Sunny Lemon Twist' (shown on page 150) and 'Sunny Gold'. These range in height from 30cm (12in) to 45cm (18in), and with their ability to resist heat and drought are excellent for the late-summer garden. They also make good cut flowers.

shrubby perennial that grows happily from self-sown seeds. An excellent foliage plant, from early spring to first frosts haloragis makes a small spreading mound of tiny, serrated leaves in a rich burnished copper, like an old penny.

Margery Fish writes admiringly of *Commelina coelestis* in *A Flower for Every Day*; she says, 'The small intensely blue flowers can be very telling and give a fillip to a tame planting. It doesn't really need another colour to enhance its beauty, although blush pink or lemon yellow could be used.' (I'm not convinced about the pink and yellow companions.) This commelina has white-flowered sister, but they are both smaller-flowered than their showier relative. Add nasturtiums, morning glory and the magical sunflower to bring together a planting scheme that will fill the final days of summer with all the light and warmth the garden can muster.

Among these dazzling Latin flowers are the colours which will also lighten the sumptuous depths of late summer's ripe tones, a fact the late Henry Mitchell, American

such colours as straw yellow, 'a color that hardly anybody starts off admiring – is one of the most useful of all colors'; it, and also pale magenta, make the dark colours 'come alive'.

Annuals and biennials are the fireworks of the garden – colourful explosions bursting on the garden scene in waves of ever-deepening colour, providing us with so much more than visual pleasure. While plant breeders and nurserymen have been focused on introducing ever more and rarer perennials, the humble annual may seem by comparison to have been ignored – undervalued and under-used, confined to windowboxes and border edgings. Perhaps this book will encourage you to rediscover the annuals and biennials you grew as a child, to experience anew the satisfaction that comes from growing a magnificent flower from seed and to awaken the creativity we all possess in some measure, blending the flower colour, shape and texture we find stored in summer's jewel box.

LEFT *Annuals in a garden add an element of uncluttered simplicity, of an almost ethereal lightness. A perennial border lacking annuals can appear lumpen, the clumps of flowers unbroken and their colours isolated from each other. Sprinkle over some annual seeds, and the picture changes, shapes meld and colours relate to each other in a most satisfying and intriguing manner as each simple blossom beckons us closer.*

RIGHT *Annuals and biennials are also capable of injecting drama into a garden scene, by their colour – like this flame-red dahlia – or by their stature, like the biennial* Angelica gigas; *both are seen here in a most strident and demanding combination.*

gardening correspondent for the *Washington Post*, pointed out in his book *The Essential Earthman*. He noted that dark mahogany, mellow bronze and sultry crimsons are enticing colours, but can be depressing if used to the exclusion of other colours, 'and what is strangest of all they become invisible at thirty feet'. How true! They seem to melt into their own shadows. Mitchell advised avoiding this by using

RIGHT *Sunflowers remain the most emblematic annual in the garden. They have been revered by generations of gardeners, artists and poets for their constancy, turning always to face the sun, tracing its path across the sky and its rising and setting with the opening and closing of their petals.*

The poet Robert Bridges captured this sentiment and the closing days of summer with his poem 'The Garden in September'. It opens:

> *'Now thin mists temper the*
> *   slow-ripening beams*
> *Of the September sun:*
> *   his golden gleams*
> *On gaudy flowers shine,*
> *   that prank the rows*
> *Of high-grown hollyhocks,*
> *   and all tall shows*
> *That Autumn flaunteth in his*
> *   bushy bowers;*
> *Where tomtits, hanging from the*
> *   drooping heads*
> *Of giant sunflowers, peck the*
> *   nutty seeds . . .'*

Just as the sunflower signals the end of day, it indicates the drawing in of summer evenings, and the final glory of an annual summer garden.

BIBLIOGRAPHY

These classic gardening texts are available from second-hand antiquarian bookshops, or sometimes from libraries. Reprint and facsimile editions have also been produced over the years, so look out for them when scouring dusty bookshelves.

The English Flower Garden William Robinson, John Murray 1883

The Wild Garden William Robinson, John Murray 1870

The Garden Manual The Cottage Gardener 1868

Pot Pourri From a Surrey Garden Mrs C.W. Earle, Smith Elder 1895

Gardening for Ladies Jane Loudon, John Murray 1841

The Scented Garden E. Sinclair Rohde, Medici Society 1931

Annuals and Biennials Gertrude Jekyll, Country Life Library 1916

Delightes For Ladies Sir Hugh Plat (facsimile ed. Crosby Lockwood 1948)

Amateur's Flower Garden Shirley Hibberd, Collingridge 1897

Recently published books that I particularly recommend, for practical, useful, inspirationtional, and expert advice on gardening generally:

Creative Vegetable Gardening Joy Larkcom, Mitchell Beazley, 1997

The Essential Earthman Henry Mitchell, Indiana University Press, 1981

Chez Panisse Vegetables Alice Waters, Harper Collins 1996

Gardening with Grasses Piet Oudolf and Michael King, Frances Lincoln, 1996 (originally published as *Prachtig Gras* Terra, Netherlands 1996)

The New Perennial Garden Noel Kingsbury, Frances Lincoln, 1996

The Art of Planting Graham Stuart Thomas, Dent 1984

The City and Town Gardener Linda Yang, Random House 1995

Warm-Climate Gardening Barbara Pleasant, Garden Way/Storey 1993

Foreign Language Publications:

Spelen met de Natuur (Playing with Nature) Henk Gerritsen, Terra, Netherlands, 1993

Tuinieren uit de Kunst (Gardening with Art) Ton der Linden, Terra, Netherlands, 1995

Nieuwe Bloemen, Nieuwe Tuinen (New Plants, New Gardens) Michael King, Terra, Netherlands, 1997

ACKNOWLEDGEMENTS

Modern gardening books could not exist without the generous cooperation of the many garden-owners and designers who allow writers and photographers into their gardens. The photographic credits compiled by Marijke say who these kind people are and I would like to add my heartfelt thanks to hers. I hope they will enjoy this book as much as I have enjoyed their gardens.

My thanks also to Martin Thrower at Thompson and Morgan for identifying the cultivars and species featured; before I embarked on this text, annuals and biennials were most familiar to me by their common names only. I've learned many, but could still do better, I'm sure.

Anna Mumford, Alison Myer and Susie Hallam at David and Charles have been a tremendous support, and I am deeply grateful to them, and also to Dick Malt, whose design talents have made planning this book a real pleasure – it wouldn't exist without them either!

This book is for my mother, Theresa Reuss, who gave me the zinnia seeds all those years ago, and thereby sowed my love of gardens and gardening.

INDEX